Cambridge Elements

Elements in Child Development
edited by
Marc H. Bornstein
National Institute of Child Health and Human Development, Bethesda
Institute for Fiscal Studies, London
UNICEF, New York City

EARLY CHILDHOOD AND DIGITAL MEDIA

Rachel Barr
Georgetown University
Heather Kirkorian
University of Wisconsin
Sarah Coyne
Brigham Young University
Jenny Radesky
University of Michigan

CAMBRIDGE
UNIVERSITY PRESS

Shaftesbury Road, Cambridge CB2 8EA, United Kingdom

One Liberty Plaza, 20th Floor, New York, NY 10006, USA

477 Williamstown Road, Port Melbourne, VIC 3207, Australia

314–321, 3rd Floor, Plot 3, Splendor Forum, Jasola District Centre, New Delhi – 110025, India

103 Penang Road, #05–06/07, Visioncrest Commercial, Singapore 238467

Cambridge University Press is part of Cambridge University Press & Assessment, a department of the University of Cambridge.

We share the University's mission to contribute to society through the pursuit of education, learning and research at the highest international levels of excellence.

www.cambridge.org
Information on this title: www.cambridge.org/9781009479301

DOI: 10.1017/9781108885751

When citing this work, please include a reference to the DOI 10.1017/9781108885751

First published 2024

A catalogue record for this publication is available from the British Library.

ISBN 978-1-009-47930-1 Hardback
ISBN 978-1-108-79456-5 Paperback
ISSN 2632-9948 (online)
ISSN 2632-993X (print)

Early Childhood and Digital Media

Elements in Child Development

DOI: 10.1017/9781108885751
First published online: March 2024

Rachel Barr
Georgetown University

Heather Kirkorian
University of Wisconsin

Sarah Coyne
Brigham Young University

Jenny Radesky
University of Michigan

Author for correspondence: Rachel Barr, rfb5@georgetown.edu

Abstract: Screen time, defined as estimates of child time spent with digital media, is considered harmful to very young children. At the same time, the use of digital media by children under 5 years of age has increased dramatically, and with the advent of mobile and streaming media can occur anywhere and at any time. Digital media have become an integral part of family life. Imprecise global screen time estimates do not capture multiple factors that shape family media ecology. In this Element, we discuss the need to shift the lens from screen time measures to measures of family media ecology, describe the new Dynamic, Relational, Ecological Approach to Media Effects Research (DREAMER) framework, and more comprehensive digital media assessments. We conclude this Element with a roadmap for future research using the DREAMER framework to better understand how digital media use is associated with child outcomes.

Keywords: early childhood, digital media, family media ecology, media content, media context

ISBNs: 9781009479301 (HB), 9781108794565 (PB), 9781108885751 (OC)
ISSNs: 2632-9948 (online), 2632-993X (print)

Contents

1 Introduction

Digital media are so pervasive that they are a fundamental part of the context in which child development occurs. Decades of research have made one thing clear: Digital media use and its effects were examined as a monolithic measure which does not capture the complexity of the current digital media landscape. For this reason, scientists and policymakers alike have called for more rigorous research on children and media (Markey, 2018; Radesky et al., 2016a; Radesky & Hiniker, 2022; Reid Chassiakos et al., 2016) to inform both federal regulations regarding child technology products and to provide guidance to parents of young children. Researchers have frequently used global measures that ask parents to estimate the amount of children's time spent viewing media – colloquially known as "screen time" – in a typical day or week. Screen time has been negatively associated with many child development outcomes (e.g., Christakis et al., 2018; Madigan et al., 2020; van den Heuvel et al., 2019). However, the use of global estimates leads to coarse and simplistic recommendations about reducing screen time that may not work for all and may not address why digital media are being used by the family. Capturing both the specificity and the complexity of the family media ecology would inform more precise guidance and intervention. For example, if sleep is disrupted because digital media are viewed immediately before bedtime, the solution may be moving the time that digital media are viewed. It is also necessary to consider everyday activities beyond media use to assess how media may either displace those activities or potentially augment them.

In this Element, we summarize what is known about family media ecology during early childhood and describe limitations in the current literature of how digital media use is studied and conceptualized. Based on our review, we argue that the approach to media effects research with children 5 years and under needs to pivot. The Dynamic, Relational, Ecological Approach to Media Effects Research (DREAMER) framework arose out of our current review of the media effects research literature on children 5 years and under. We describe findings of associations between screen time and child outcomes and point out the gaps in this literature which necessitate a move to a new framework. Specifically, we describe the DREAMER framework that takes a dynamic and relational approach to media effects research that moves beyond more static conceptualizations of the associations between media use and child outcomes that have dominated the field. We also highlight gaps in measurement that are needed in order to test the DREAMER framework.

In this Element, we first review the empirical literature on the amount, content, and context of media use that produce wide variations in family media experiences. We argue that these variations necessitate a shift in lens away from traditional screen time paradigms toward understanding the family media ecology. Next, we summarize some existing theories that have tried to address the complexity of media exposure as well as theoretical frameworks that have not yet been applied to this topic but have the potential to inform a more comprehensive framework. Following this theoretical review, we introduce the DREAMER framework to illustrate how prior theories can be expanded to consider dynamic and relational processes that unfold across time to better represent the family media ecology. We also present a case study to illustrate the DREAMER framework based on shifts in family media ecology that occurred during the COVID-19 pandemic. Next, we highlight limitations in current measures of children's digital media use and advocate for more comprehensive measurement approaches that are needed to better capture the family media ecology and to test the DREAMER framework. We conclude with future directions to test the DREAMER framework aimed at better understanding children growing up in the digital world.

2 Review of the Literature: Shifting the Lens from "Screen Time" to "Family Media Ecology"

2.1 Traditional Measures of Screen Time

Traditionally, research on media effects in children 5 and under has focused on screen time, often characterized as the amount of time children spend viewing screen media in a typical day or week. Although patterns are similar across many countries (e.g., Bellagamba et al., 2021; Goh et al., 2016; Gueron-Sela et al., 2023; Sundqvist et al., 2021; Takahashi et al., 2023), screen time is most studied in the U.S. context. Most U.S. families with young children own a smartphone (97%) or tablet (78%), and nearly half (46%) of 2- to 4-year-olds had their own mobile devices (smartphone or tablet) in 2020 (Rideout & Robb, 2020). Due to the increased accessibility of mobile devices, mobile use increased dramatically in the last decade. Additionally, mobile device use differs across demographics such as race. For example, mobile device use by White children 8 years and younger increased from an average of 4 minutes per day in 2011 to 37 minutes per day in 2020, while mobile device use for Black children increased from 8 minutes per day in 2011 to 104 minutes per day in 2020 (Rideout & Robb, 2020). Among low-income households, as many as 75% of young children own their own tablet, and most parents own smartphones (Kabali et al., 2015). The manner that young children view media has changed since the rapid adoption of mobile devices and increased availability of broadband internet. The proportion of time spent on online platforms like YouTube (37%) and streaming content (like Netflix, 29%) is higher than live or on demand television (23%; Radesky et al., 2020c; Rideout & Robb, 2020). Daily screen time also increases with child age, averaging 49 minutes for children 0–2 years old, 2.5 hours for children 2–4 years old, just over 3 hours for children 5–8 years old, and about 5.5 hours for children 8–12 years old (Rideout & Robb, 2020; Rideout et al., 2022). During the COVID-19 pandemic, some young children also had access to school-issued devices for virtual or hybrid learning that has helped shape their media habits (Katz et al., 2021).

Prior research has done much to identify correlates and stability in screen time. Decades of research have examined associations between TV viewing and child outcomes (Reid Chassiakos et al., 2016). For example, more screen time during early childhood is associated with attentional and self-regulation problems (e.g., Barr et al., 2010a; Christakis et al., 2018; Ribner et al., 2021), delays in language development (e.g., Christakis et al., 2009; Madigan et al., 2020; Sundqvist et al., 2023; Takahashi et al., 2023; van den Heuvel et al., 2019), obesity (Ramirez-Coronel et al., 2023; Robinson et al., 2017), and sleep dysregulation (Cheung et al., 2017; Garrison et al., 2011; Lund et al., 2021; Mallawaarachchi et al. 2022). More screen time is also correlated with poorer social skills and school readiness (e.g., Barr et al., 2010a; Barr & Linebarger, 2017; Reid Chassiakos et al., 2016). For example, Madigan and colleagues (2020) used data from the Strengths and Difficulties Questionnaire, a clinical screening tool, to demonstrate longitudinal associations between overall screen time and developmental risk, but processes that explain the association between screen time and risk remain unclear. There is a similarly robust (albeit newer) literature on time spent on video games, social media, and smartphone use; however, this literature is primarily focused on older children and adolescents (Barr & Linebarger, 2017; Blumberg & Brooks, 2017).

The rigor of prior research on young children's screen time is limited by measurement methods that have not kept pace with the evolution of technology. Amid such ambiguity, parents, educators, and policymakers often remain polarized about the adoption of digital devices, acting with either extreme concern or overly optimistic enthusiasm (Lauricella et al., 2017). The need for more rigor and more practical guidance for parents requires a reconceptualization of young children's screen time that reflects the complexity of children's digital worlds.

2.2 The Family Media Ecology

Technology is the leading reason U.S. parents believe parenting is different today than it was 20 years ago (Auxier et al., 2020). This is true among the 68% of parents who feel parenting has become more difficult and the 7% who feel it has become easier. Research examining the role of media similarly illustrates the rapidly changing experiences of parenting in the digital age. The complexity in the environment is perhaps because of the degree of digital media saturation levels in homes, the proliferation of different internet-connected devices and platforms used by (but not always designed for) young children, and increasing presence of marketing, user-generated content, and automated systems. The sole use of screen time as an outcome measure is no longer adequate to understand the processes that explain the effects of digital media use on children, given a changing media landscape and a growing awareness that the overall family media ecology must be considered. In addition to the amount of time spent using media and other family activities, family media ecology comprises a set of factors that both directly and indirectly influence all members of the family system, including children, via both the content and context of exposure. It is now recognized that developmental outcomes are predicted by not only the amount of time that children interact with digital media, but also how each family member is using media and what type of media they are engaging with (Barr & Linebarger, 2017).

We use the term "ecology" to represent the multiple interrelated family members, behaviors, and processes that exist in households and influence each other in dynamic and bidirectional ways over time. For example, parents' media usage on all devices (television, computers, smartphones, and tablets) is one of the strongest predictors of children's screen use behaviors from infancy to 8 years of age (Anderson & Hanson, 2017; Bleakley et al., 2013; Connell et al., 2015; Goh et al., 2016; Lauricella et al., 2015; Nikken & Schols, 2015; Pempek & McDaniel, 2016). This association is explained by informal learning and norm-setting, how family routines are structured, and the functional uses of media in households (e.g., for entertainment, for stress relief). Factors considered as constituents of the family media ecology include individual parent characteristics, such as parent mental health, which is linked with children's media exposure (e.g., Bank et al., 2012; Conners et al., 2007; Coyne et al., 2021; Goh et al., 2016; McDaniel & Radesky, 2020; Nikken & Schols, 2015; Pempek & McDaniel, 2016; Tombeau Cost et al., 2020). Structural forces surrounding the family, such as household income (Anand & Krosnick, 2005; Przybylski & Weinstein, 2017), and race and ethnicity-related processes, such as marginalization (Calvert et al., 2005; Connell et al., 2015; Lauricella et al., 2015; Rideout & Robb, 2020), also shape the family media ecology. Specifically, low-income minority children are exposed to more screen time, than are children from higher-income households (Anand & Krosnick, 2005; Calvert et al., 2005; Goh et al., 2016; Przybylski & Weinstein, 2017). Conversely, higher parental education and family wealth are associated with lower child media usage, amounting to a difference of 30 minutes per day in children 0 to 8 years

(Rideout, 2017) and about 2 hours per day for 8- to 18-year-olds (Rideout, 2015) compared to families with lower education and wealth.

In the sections that follow, we illustrate that digital media effects are not invariant; they depend on the media content and design (e.g., Barr et al., 2010a, b; Barr et al., 2020; Barr & Linebarger, 2017; Bus et al., 2020; Linebarger et al., 2014; Wright et al., 2001) and several aspects of media use context related to the family media ecology (e.g., Kirkorian et al., 2009; Kirkorian et al., 2019; Neuman et al., 2020; Zack & Barr, 2016). We discuss each in turn.

2.3 Digital Media Content

Content has been shown to be a better predictor of outcomes than screen time alone (Barr & Linebarger, 2017). Generally, poorer quality content is associated with negative outcomes and better quality with positive outcomes for children. Content analyses have provided detailed information about media features that promote or hinder learning and other social and emotional outcomes (e.g., Fenstermacher et al., 2010a; Hirsh-Pasek et al., 2015; Linebarger et al., 2017; Meyer et al., 2021) and predict academic developmental trajectories (Anderson et al., 2001). In this section, we summarize the comparatively large body of literature on content and design considerations for traditional screen media (e.g., broadcast television and movies) and the emerging literature on interactive touchscreen media (e.g., mobile applications, electronic books).

2.3.1 Traditional Screen Media

Video content remains the most common form of digital media for children 5 years and under, making up approximately 73% of viewing time, although it is increasingly viewed in streaming formats on multiple devices, from traditional family television sets, to tablets and smartphones (Rideout & Robb, 2020). Educational television programs designed explicitly for young children (e.g., Sesame Workshop and PBS Kids programming) have been associated with greater school readiness and better long-term educational trajectories, particularly for children who live in lower-income homes and children of color (e.g., Anderson et al., 2001; Linebarger et al., 2014; Wright et al., 2001). Video content may also promote positive outcomes via prosocial behaviors that media characters model. Educational and prosocial content often models healthy emotion regulation strategies (e.g., Daniel Tiger's Neighborhood; Malti & Dys, 2018; Rasmussen et al., 2016). Exposure to well-designed children's programming is associated with long-term positive outcomes for language and executive functioning (Anderson et al., 2001; Barr et al., 2010a; Linebarger & Walker, 2005; Linebarger & Vaala, 2010). Even in infancy, children are shown to be attentive to media content that matches their interests and is meaningful to them (Nikken & Schols, 2015). Well-designed video content can also inspire high-quality parent–child interaction when parents watch together with their children (Pempek et al., 2011).

Conversely, poorer cognitive and emotion regulation profiles in children have been associated with lower-quality content and exposure to adult-directed or background television (Barr et al., 2010a; Schmidt et al., 2008; Linebarger et al., 2014). Prior research indicates longitudinal associations of longer daily television viewing duration and low-quality media content with toddler externalizing behavior (Tomopolous et al., 2007), preschooler behavioral problems (Verlinden et al., 2012), and lower early childhood psychosocial well-being (Pagani et al., 2010). Exposure to high levels of background TV, much of which may be adult-directed rather than child-centered and educational, has been associated with later emotional reactivity, externalizing behavior, and aggression in toddlers (Chonchaiya et al., 2015) and lower executive function in preschoolers (Barr et al., 2010a).

2.3.2 Interactive Touchscreen Media

Touchscreen interfaces on smartphones and tablets can also include interactivity that shapes the impact of content on children. Interactive apps and platforms provide contingent responsiveness to children's input, allowing feedback and digital scaffolding in support of curricular goals. Interactive media are likely to support children's learning when the interactive features focus on, rather than distract from, the lesson (Furenes et al., 2021; Kirkorian, 2018). Alternatively, digital interactivity in the form of extraneous audiovisual effects or advertising can distract from learning processes (Bus et al., 2020).

Hirsh-Pasek and colleagues (2015) used Science of Learning principles, which are summarized in Table 1, to describe how effective educational programming can be designed in mobile app form. Educational approaches to interactive design emphasize children's "minds-on" rather than automatic engagement, interactive features that support learning activities, meaningful curricula, and supporting social interactions around the app. In other words, the effects of interactive technology depend on the quality of content (e.g., Is the app based on an educational curriculum?) and aspects of interactive design (e.g., Do ads disrupt the play experience? Are the tasks repetitive versus "minds-on"?) (Hirsh-Pasek, et al., 2015). However, detailed coding of the top-rated or top-downloaded "educational" apps in the Google Play Store and Apple App Store demonstrated that these features occur only infrequently in commercial products (Meyer et al., 2021). Moreover, many apps and child platforms that are marketed as educational

Table 1 Science of learning pillars as characterized by Hirsh-Pasek et al. (2015).

Category	Description
Pillar 1: Active Learning	Gameplay is minds-on. It is not repetitive/ closed-loop; provides flexibility for child to generate responses; does not spoon-feed
Pillar 2: Engagement in the Learning Process	Enhancements act to support learning, do not distract from it or over gamify
Pillar 3: Meaningful learning	Content is meaningful to the child and relates to everyday life or is taught in a way that can be easily integrated
Pillar 4: Social interaction	Provides opportunities for contingent interactions with parasocial character defined as a one-sided, emotionally tinged relationships with media characters such as Elmo (Richards & Calvert, 2017), or space for co-viewer to co-play

are frequently monetized through advertisements (Meyer et al., 2018), data collection (Zhao et al., 2020), and nudges to make purchases (Radesky et al., 2022).

As with television and video content, the quality of interactive design may also shape parent–child interaction around media. The interactive design affordances and monetization of children's digital products have the potential to influence how children learn from digital media and how digital media could displace or interrupt other daily activities or relational processes. For example, observational research demonstrated that parents had difficulty getting their young child's attention (Hiniker et al., 2018b) and social reciprocity decreased (Munzer et al., 2019) when apps were fast-paced and had high levels of interactive design. In a laboratory-based experiment, toddlers showed more negativity toward their parents when prompted to transition away from a nursery rhyme app on a mobile device, compared to the same content in a print book (Munzer et al., 2021).

Interactive design features have unique implications for the types of digital media content children view. Radesky and colleagues (2020) tracked the mobile devices of preschool-aged children and found that the most commonly used media were mobile games and YouTube, which were used for an average of 1 hour per day. Such apps use multiple strategies to increase usage time and may expose infants and young children to more consumerist, age-inappropriate, and violent content (Munzer et al., 2022). The content of these channels and apps and their impact on children's development is poorly understood. Design features that merit further study include engagement-prolonging design (e.g., autoplay, behavioral reinforcement with frequent rewards) as engagement-prolonging design may be more likely to displace other important developmental opportunities for young children and may have associations with greater child behavioral difficulties when transitioning off devices (Munzer et al., 2022). However, the vast array of interactive apps, immersive games, and platforms now popular with young children poses measurement challenges as interactive design analysis is time- and labor-intensive. In addition, now that video, audio, and game content is personalized for child users through automated filtering and recommender systems, researchers need to understand how algorithmic decision-making shapes the media experience of young children.

2.4 Context of Digital Media Use

Despite the importance of context, most research focuses on child behavior and development in isolation, ignoring the ways in which children's media use is embedded within the family media ecology (Barr et al., 2020). Although there are many different contexts in which children use media, we focus on four relational and family systems contexts that are particularly important to understanding child media use within the larger family media ecology: parental mediation, technoference, motivations for using digital media, and structural factors.

2.4.1 Parental Mediation

Parental mediation strategies have been studied quite extensively. Parental mediation guides how children learn the function of media, how to operate a device, and how to interpret the content (Nikken & Schols, 2015). For mediation of television, three general categories have emerged: (1) restrictive time and content limits; (2) active parental discussion of content; and (3) co-viewing for education and entertainment (Nikken & Schols, 2015; Piotrowski, 2017; Valkenburg et al., 1999). Parents typically use restrictive media practices to limit inappropriate content, whereas they are more likely to actively mediate educational content (Nikken & Schols, 2015). Like screen time, structural factors also predict parental mediation (Connell et al., 2015; Wang et al., 2023). For example, in a study conducted in the United States, younger parents and fathers were more likely to co-engage with video games and mobile technology than older parents and mothers, and Latine/x parents were more likely to co-engage with tablet computers compared to White parents (Connell et al., 2015). Device type also matters. For instance, parents of children 8 years and younger were more likely to report co-engagement with television and books than with smartphones and tablet computers (Connell et al., 2015). Parental attitudes about media also influence mediation practices (Nikkens & Schols, 2015; Piotrowski, 2017; Valkenburg et al., 1999; Wang et al., 2023). For example, a meta-analysis of predictors of parental mediation showed that parents who had more positive and more negative attitudes toward media and had higher levels of parental involvement were more likely to engage in active mediation practices compared to parents without strong positive or negative attitudes toward media (Wang et al., 2023). The biggest predictors of restrictive media practices were child age and parent media attitudes, with more restrictive practices used for younger children and parents with more negative attitudes.

For very young children, active mediation frequently takes the form of joint media engagement (JME), defined as the extent to which parents actively engage with their children during media use (e.g., playing games together, talking about the content). JME has been examined during television viewing, e-book reading, and app use (Dore et al., 2018; Fidler et al., 2010; Lauricella et al., 2009, 2014; Zack & Barr, 2016). Learning from media during early childhood is limited by children's cognitive and memory constraints (e.g., Barr, 2013). However, high-quality JME can help overcome such constraints to increase young children's learning. For example, JME significantly increased 15-month-olds' transfer of learning from a touchscreen to the physical world (Zack & Barr, 2016). Similarly, Heimann and colleagues (2021) showed that JME also enhanced imitation learning in 2-year-olds.

JME also enhances adult–child conversations, which create new opportunities for early word learning. Lavigne and colleagues (2015) found that parents included more new words per utterance during co-viewing, and this extra vocabulary carried over after the television program ended, resulting in richer parental language during a subsequent free play episode. The authors speculated that high-quality educational content could provide parents with topics that might be of interest or model language that parents could use with their young children. Such opportunities may explain why JME appears to buffer the negative effects of early media use on children's language and literacy development (Dore et al., 2020). They may also explain why JME combined with the use of educational content is associated with greater vocabulary, whereas solitary media use is associated with mostly neutral or negative language and cognitive outcomes (Madigan et al., 2020; Sundqvist et al., 2021). For example, in a study of low-income Latine/x mothers and their children, Mendelsohn and colleagues (2010) found that the degree to which parents reported actively discussing educational media content when their children were 6 months old predicted their children's language outcomes at age 14 months. Specifically, verbal interactions during educational content at age 6 months were associated with better language outcomes at age 14 months. Similarly, Rasmussen and colleagues (2016) found that the effectiveness of a prosocial program aimed at 2- to 4-year-olds was maximized by parent reports of consistent active mediation practices in the home.

The benefits of JME for language and literacy extend to other forms of digital media use, including e-books and video chat (Krcmar & Cingel, 2014; Lauricella et al., 2014; Strouse & Ganea, 2016, 2017). For example, in an experimental study of JME during video chat, children learned more words when their caregiver engaged in JME with the child than when their caregiver did not engage in JME (Myers et al., 2018). In some cases, carefully designed digital media may deliver some of the learning enhancements provided by JME. For example, Dore et al. (2018) found that children comprehend some content from e-books using audio narration, indicating that using e-books independently may be a worthwhile activity for preliterate children while caregivers are otherwise occupied. However, results also show that children recall the most information about the e-book after reading with a parent.

Other research suggests there may be individual child differences in the benefits of JME. For example, JME disproportionately enhanced learning for children with lower vocabulary and executive functioning scores, probably because adults tailored the information to meet the needs of individual children (Strouse & Ganea, 2016). Overall, JME is likely to be highly effective and protective because learning from media is cognitively challenging and requires that children learn the features of different media types and the affordances of each device. In the face of such challenges, JME is currently the most effective way to tailor learning from media during early childhood (Barr, 2019b).

The majority of JME research focuses on parent–child media co-use. One factor that is almost entirely overlooked in this research is the role of siblings. Older siblings are likely to influence screen time and content choice. Moreover, JME patterns are likely to differ for family media use with siblings of different ages versus one-on-one parent–child interactions. Similarly, the literature rarely considers the influence of more than one caregiver, such as the degree to which parents in the same family system adopt similar media rules and practices. Going forward, media effects research could be expanded to better reflect the entire family media ecology.

2.4.2 Technoference

Technology use and the presence of technology can distract, interrupt, and intrude on parenting and parent–child interactions, which is termed technoference (e.g., McDaniel & Coyne, 2016; McDaniel & Radesky, 2018a; McDaniel, 2020).

Technoference is common across a variety of child activities (e.g., feedings/mealtimes, indoor and outdoor play). Early research on technoference focused on the impact of background television, demonstrating a decrease in the quality and quantity of parent and child play and social interactions in the presence versus absence of background television (Pempek & Kirkorian, 2020). For example, in experimental research with parents and their 12- to 36-month-old children, background television decreased parents' and children's interactions, parents' responsiveness to their children's bids for attention, and the degree to which parents actively engaged in their children's toy play (Kirkorian et al., 2009).

More recently, research has expanded to examine technoference in the context of parents' smartphone use. During parental smartphone use, examples of associated technoference include decreases in appropriate and timely responses to children's bids for attention (Abels et al., 2018; Domoff et al., 2020; Elias et al., 2021; Ewin et al., 2021; Hiniker et al., 2015; Kiefner-Burmeister et al., 2020, Vanden Abeele et al., 2020), reduced awareness of dangerous situations or injuries (Elias et al., 2021), reductions in joint play, conversations, or engagement (Ewin et al., 2021; Konrad et al., 2021b; Krapf-Bar et al., 2022; Ochoa et al., 2021; Linder et al., 2022), decreased sensitivity/warmth (Konrad et al., 2021b; Radesky et al., 2014a; Ventura et al., 2019), increased child behavior problems (Linder et al., 2022; McDaniel & Radesky, 2018b; Radesky et al., 2014a; Vanden Abeele et al., 2020), and poorer language learning (Reed et al., 2017). For example, in observations of caregivers and young children in fast food restaurants, many parents showed high attentional absorption with smartphones, which co-occurred with less parent–child conversation and more child behavior escalation (Radesky et al., 2014a). In another study, when mothers used smartphones around their children, the mothers exhibited less frequent verbal and nonverbal interactions with their young children during meals (Radesky et al., 2015) and, when interviewed, displayed diminished capacity for mentalization, or perspective-taking, about their child (Radesky et al., 2018b). In addition, parent phone use during mealtime interactions is associated with lower use of positive feeding practices like responsiveness to child hunger and fullness cues, less frequent modeling of healthy eating behaviors, and greater use of less desirable feeding practices such as use of food to regulate children's emotions or pressuring children to eat (Robinson et al., 2022; Ventura & Teitelbaum 2017; Ventura et al., 2019; Vik et al., 2021). Associations between technoference and child characteristics may be bidirectional: In a longitudinal study of parent technoference, child externalizing behavior predicted parent technoference just as strongly as parent technoference predicted increases in child externalizing behavior (McDaniel & Radesky, 2018a).

A number of relational processes underlie the reciprocal association between technoference and child behavior. As noted earlier, one likely mechanism is disruption in parents' emotional availability and their appropriate and timely responses to children's bids for attention (e.g., Domoff et al., 2020; Hiniker et al., 2015; Kirkorian et al., 2009). During observational studies researchers noted that parents often portrayed a flat affect when absorbed in mobile device content. This flat expressionless face resembles a classic still-face (Konrad et al., 2021a, b; Krapf-Bar et al., 2022; Myruski et al., 2018). Experimental studies have shown that infants find such expressionless flat affect aversive and often attempt to regain an adult's attention via increased vocalization (Goldstein et al., 2009). Eventually, infants may learn that the use of the smartphone is a cue that their mothers are unavailable and wait to reengage only when the smartphone is no longer in use (Konrad et al., 2021b). Researchers have posited that withdrawal of positive affect during phone use might be a potential explanatory mechanism for the negative outcomes associated with technoference. To test this hypothesis, researchers designed experimental studies. For example, Krapf-Bar et al. (2022) conducted a study of the relation between mobile phone disruptions and joint activity between mothers and infants at 12 months. Mobile phone disruptions due to texting were more likely to disrupt the formation and duration of joint attention and joint activity between mothers and their 1-year-olds than a social disruption caused by an experimenter talking to the mother. Another study compared differences between smartphone text disruptions and a non-digital disruption via a paper-and-pencil survey (Konrad et al., 2021b). In both interruption scenarios, maternal responsiveness and infant positive affect decreased, suggesting that it is not only technology disruptions that interrupt social exchanges. Higher levels of absorption during the task were related to lower levels of responsiveness to both digital and nondigital distractions. However, while both technological and analog behaviors may disrupt interactions, smartphone use may be more frequent and disruptive due to the frequency of notifications and ubiquity of parental smartphone use, leading to larger cumulative effects over time (McDaniel, 2021).

It has not been established whether the effects of technoference on parent–child interactions differ as a function of the content and context of parental phone use. Activities such as parental social media use or checking and responding to work emails may result in higher levels of absorption, whereas brief glances at notifications may not interfere with ongoing parent–child interactions. Furthermore, individual differences in how parents split their attention between their children and the digital screen are likely to influence the degree to which the phone use and background television are experienced as technoference (Kirkorian et al., 2019; Konrad et al., 2021a). Beyond the amount of overall household media use, parent's own media use patterns and their motivations and responses to media are often overlooked. Millennial and Gen

Z parents have grown up with access to a wide array of media resources. This technology use may also support parents through mechanisms such as stress relief or access to support or resources (Radesky et al., 2016c; Torres et al., 2021). Specifically, smartphone use during breastfeeding is common, and although parents report they felt guilty, they also report benefits such as distraction, connection with others, or staying awake at night which is associated with persistence in breastfeeding (Coyne et al., 2022a). Additional research is needed to track the long-term effects of technoference on children.

2.4.3 Motivations for Media Use

Family digital media use does not occur at random. Instead, it is often motivated by parents' needs and goals for themselves and their young children. Yet, research often overlooks the reasons that parents use technology, and parents are seldom asked why they use media (Nikken, 2019; Nikken & Schols, 2015). When asked, parents of young children report using media to meet a wide range of needs (Nikken, 2019). Commonly reported reasons for child media use include keeping the child busy or entertained when the parent is occupied, taking a break from childrearing, and using media to regulate children's behavior or emotions (Nikken, 2019). Parents' motivations for media use may shape children's media exposure. For example, Nikken and Schols (2015) reported that children spend significantly more time using mobile devices and have more electronic screens in their bedrooms when their parents endorse the statement that digital media provide a moment of rest.

The fact that digital media serve so many functions might explain why children's digital media use is predicted by parenting stress (Madigan et al., 2020), maternal depression (Bank et al., 2012; Coyne et al., 2021; Pempek & McDaniel, 2016), poor maternal relational well-being (Tombeau Cost et al., 2020), and low child self-regulation (Coyne et al., 2021; McDaniel & Radesky, 2020; Nabi & Krcmar, 2016). The many functions of media use may also partially explain why media use is higher among lower-resourced and minority families (Rideout & Robb, 2020), and why media use was higher during the COVID-19 pandemic than before the pandemic (Hartshorne et al., 2021). Indeed, some scholars have called for reframing child media use as an indicator of parental distress (Hartshorne et al., 2021). The relation between parents' mental health and family media use is not straightforward. Researchers have found some motivations for media use to be constructive in meeting parents' needs in supportive ways (e.g., bonding over shared media, connecting with faraway family). For instance, depressed or highly stressed mothers choose more child-directed, educational media than their non-depressed or less-stressed counterparts (Bank et al., 2012; Pempek & McDaniel, 2016), suggesting that depressed or stressed mothers may use media to provide cognitive stimulation for their children. More information about the types of media and media use practices associated with contextual stressors is needed.

Other investigators have found that some types of media use may displace high-quality parent–child interactions (Kirkorian et al., 2009, 2019; Radesky et al., 2015). Some parental motivations for media use (e.g., to enable parents' escape from stress or parenting, to regulate children's emotions or behavior) may be problematic for early socioemotional development (Coyne et al., 2021; McDaniel & Radesky, 2018). Using media to calm young children may be particularly problematic for the development of self-regulation by removing opportunities for children to learn and practice self-regulatory skills (Coyne et al., 2021; McDaniel & Radesky, 2018). Such regulatory uses of mobile devices to calm children have been associated cross-sectionally with social-emotional delays (Radesky et al., 2016d) and worse emotional knowledge and reactivity (Coyne et al., 2023b). Longitudinal findings are fewer and provide mixed results. Some studies have shown that regulatory media use predicts negative outcomes of higher emotional reactivity (Gordon-Hacker & Gueron-Sela, 2020). In contrast, other studies have demonstrated that regulatory media use predicts positive outcomes of higher levels of empathy in preschoolers (Coyne et al., 2023b).

The reasons parents use digital media for and around their young children may shape the content and context of media use. For example, using digital media to escape or regulate might lead to more solitary media use, less joint media engagement, and selection of streaming media or apps with exploitative features that keep children engaged for prolonged periods of time (Radesky et al., 2022; Radesky & Hiniker, 2022). The extent to which digital media use disrupts positive parent–child interactions may explain why children's self-regulation has been linked to some types of media use but not others. For example, TV viewing during infancy and toddlerhood, especially viewing adult-directed or violent content, is associated with children's worse emotion and attention regulation (Barr et al., 2010a; Gueron-Sela & Gordon-Hacker, 2020; McDaniel & Radesky, 2018; Zimmerman & Christakis, 2007).

Finally, the literature points to bidirectional relations between parents' mental health, parent and child digital media use, and child behavior. That is, more challenging child temperament (i.e., negative affect, low effortful control) predicts increased parental stress, in turn predicting increased digital media use for parents and children (Coyne et al., 2021; McDaniel & Radesky, 2018, 2020; Shin et al., 2021). The state of the research underscores the importance of the early caregiving environment for the development of self-regulation and that media may be one feasible target for intervention. There are limitations in the extant literature such that there is little research predicting positive media motivations (e.g., to bond and relax together). Researchers have also examined how motivations for child and family media use and the type of media content chosen may fluctuate day-to-day, or even hour-to-hour (Coyne et al., 2021). These decisions may depend on the stress and well-being of the parent and the behavior and temperament of the child. However, these moment-to-moment decisions have received little empirical attention. Commonly used parent-report measures, which ask parents about their typical behaviors over two or more weeks, may lack precision. Collectively, this research suggests a link between parents' own needs and their use of digital media with and around children, but much remains to be learned about the short-term dynamic processes that shape media decisions for children in the moment and how such decisions may accumulate over time to affect longer-term child outcomes.

2.4.4 Structural Factors

Structural factors, such as income inequality, institutional racism (e.g., in housing or educational opportunity), and disinvestment in marginalized communities, shape multiple child development outcomes through the opportunities available to families. Parents who use more digital media often come from low-SES backgrounds (Lauricella et al., 2015; Rideout & Robb, 2020), suggesting there may be functional uses of media for families with fewer resources compared with middle- or upper-SES families. Clear evidence is emerging of disparities in access to quality content and/or stable internet connections by SES (socioeconomic status) (Katz et al., 2019, 2021; Ramsetty et al., 2020; Sen & Tucker, 2020). For example, children of parents with a high school degree had significantly higher mobile device use (155.2 minutes/day) compared to parents with an advanced degree (82.3 minutes/day), were 8 times more likely to use YouTube (Radesky et al., 2020c), and had a two- to threefold higher rate of using apps that illegally collect private data (e.g., device identifiers that marketers use for behavioral advertising, Zhao et al., 2020). Communities of color are more likely to be targets of marketing of unhealthy products and financially exploitative services (Radesky et al., 2020b), which serve to maintain inequities in access to quality input. SES and related psychosocial constructs are often examined as confounders or moderators in child media research, but research also needs to consider the ways that structural inequality is interwoven with family opportunity, media ecology, and the digital ecosystem itself.

2.5 Child Outcomes: A Focus on Content and Context

Here we describe associations between media use and more specific outcomes illustrating the importance of considering the content and context of exposure. Clearly this review does not encompass all relevant child outcomes, but we highlight a few that tend to be more specific to early childhood and that have been studied extensively. In every case, associations between digital media use and child outcomes differ based on the media content, the context of media use, or both. We also focus on lessons learned from media use data collected during the COVID-19 pandemic.

2.5.1 Sleep

Systematic reviews provide consistent evidence that exposure to screen-based media in infancy, toddlerhood, and early childhood is negatively associated with sleep duration (Lund et al., 2021; Moorman et al., 2019; Zhang et al., 2021). Mallawaarachchi et al.'s (2022) meta-analysis reported that poorer sleep outcomes were associated with everyday use of a tablet or smartphone (see also Cheung et al., 2017; Chindamo et al., 2019). Some studies have shown that higher levels of screen exposure were associated with prolonged sleep onset latency (Bellagamba et al., 2021; Cheung et al., 2017; Xu et al., 2016). In a longitudinal study that controlled for several demographic variables, Benita and colleagues (2020) found that parental use of media to calm 22-month-old infants predicted longer latency to fall asleep at 26 months and that more media exposure at 22 months was associated with less nighttime sleep at 26 months. Findings on sleep fragmentation (number of times a child wakes during the night) and clinically meaningful sleep problems are mixed (Bellagamba et al., 2021; Cheung et al., 2017; Xu et al., 2016; Zhang et al., 2019).

Bellagamba and colleagues (2021) provided evidence for the importance of digital media context when examining associations between digital media use and child sleep. These researchers collected data using a media questionnaire and the Brief Screening Questionnaire for Infant Sleep Problems (BISQ; Sadeh, 2004) from parents of children under 3 years of age. The BISQ measures the estimated amount of time an infant sleeps during the night and naps during the day, the number of times an infant wakes during the night, and sleep problems. Media use was associated with less mature sleep patterns. Critically, these associations differed based on several contextual factors. For example, when there were more devices available in the household, young children went to bed later and had less nighttime sleep and more daytime sleep. Parents' motivations for digital media use also mattered. When parents used media to occupy the child and when they reported higher overall levels of media use, children also had later bedtimes and less nighttime sleep.

Given rapid changes in sleep patterns during early childhood, findings also vary as a function of the age of the child as well as the device type. Researchers have posited that the timing of exposure is important as media before bedtime might increase behavioral arousal or displace parent–child interaction during sleep routines, both of which might disrupt sleep onset and quality (Cheung et al., 2017; Mallawaarachchi et al., 2022; Lund et al., 2021). Longitudinal and experimental research that considers the content and the context (e.g., timing of media exposure) is needed to disentangle these potential processes. Advanced techniques, including actigraphy and passive sensing, should be used to detect how sleep is disrupted and how sleep patterns change as a function of child age. Such methods could detect whether sleep onset is disrupted by different forms of content, or whether there are changes in nighttime wakings due to notifications or media use during the night. Interventions would then be tailored based on these findings.

2.5.2 Language

Viewing low-quality TV content is associated with language delays in young children, whereas viewing high-quality educational programs is protective and associated with higher vocabulary (Celenn Yoldas & Ozmert, 2021; Jing et al., 2023; Madigan et al., 2020). High-quality educational content can promote language development through children's word-learning and parents' infant-directed speech. For example, Linebarger and Walker (2005) analyzed whether televised content was associated with vocabulary trajectories between 6 and 30 months of age, collecting data at 3-month intervals. Educational content, interactive narratives, and content with familiar characters were associated with vocabulary growth. This finding may be due to word learning from media designed to teach vocabulary, as evidenced by a meta-analysis (Jing et al., 2023). Furthermore, unlike adult-directed television (Pempek et al., 2014), infant-directed videos specifically designed to model positive parent–infant interactions succeed in increasing parent–child interaction quality (Pempek et al., 2011) and the lexical diversity of parents' infant-directed speech (Lavigne et al., 2015).

Conversely, media exposure affects the language environment and often reduces child–adult interaction because it does not facilitate socially contingent conversational turns with a language partner whose responses are immediate, reliable, and accurate in content and relevance (Anderson & Hanson, 2017). As described earlier, family media use can create digital distraction that affects the amount and quality of family interactions. Such technoference has implications for young children's language development. For example, brief interruptions to parent–child interactions via a phone call disrupted word learning in toddlers (Reed et al., 2017). JME has the potential to foster greater parent–child interaction. However, while some parents provide descriptions and even pause videos to discuss content with some success, such language-rich interactions tend to occur less often than during face-to-face interactions (Strouse et al., 2013). Without the support of an active mediating adult, media alone cannot scaffold the content to meet the specific needs of very young children.

Researchers hypothesize that solitary use of media by the parent or the child might be negatively associated with the child's language development (Dore et al., 2020). However, if parents engage in JME and discuss the media content with the child either during media use or in follow-up activities, then such experiences might enhance language outcomes. For example, parents of 2-year-olds completed a media questionnaire and a child vocabulary measure (Sundqvist et al., 2021). Researchers also provided audio recording devices to parents who recorded the auditory environment of the child. The researchers found that child vocabulary decreased as a function of parent-reported screen time for the child, and child vocabulary was lower for parents who indicated they used digital media during child routines (Sundqvist et al., 2021). On the other hand, positive linguistic parental strategies, such as interactional turn-taking with the child, JME, shared book reading, and use of mental state language were positively associated with children's vocabulary development (Sundqvist et al., 2021). JME via video chat provides an even more enriched context for early word learning (Myers et al., 2018). In sum, the quality of parent–child verbal interactions surrounding digital media use is the key predictor of child language outcomes.

2.5.3 Executive Function and Attention

Longitudinal studies have revealed complex patterns among digital media use, attention, and executive function outcomes. In a longitudinal study, higher levels of household media usage including maternal mobile usage and background televisions at 18 months predicted worse infant attention at 22 months (Gueron-Sela & Gordon-Hacker, 2020). In this study, in addition to a traditional measure of child screen time, the investigators collected measures of the family media ecology, including parental use of digital media to regulate child behavior, use of background television, and maternal mobile usage. They analyzed their data as a function of each media type and created a cumulative measure which was a proportion of the maximum value of each media type. Concurrent measures of focused attention were not associated with cumulative family media use. However, higher cumulative family media use at 18 months was associated with poorer focused attention at 22 months and at 26 months. Similarly, in a short-term longitudinal study of 2- to 3-year-olds, which controlled for a range of covariates including verbal ability, McHarg and colleagues (2020) found no concurrent association between screen time and executive function; however, screen time at age 2 negatively predicted child executive function at age 3.

There is some evidence that media content may moderate associations between digital media use and cognitive development. For instance, exposure to adult-directed (but not child-directed) television at age 1 year negatively predicted executive function at age 4 years (Barr et al., 2010a). Similarly, viewing violent or non-violent entertainment television (but not educational television) before age 3 years predicted attention problems at age 7 years (Zimmerman & Christakis, 2007). Together, these findings suggest that negative associations between early television viewing and later attention and executive function depend on digital media content, with child-directed and educational programs buffering the negative associations seen with adult-directed or non-educational content. However, these studies did not include other contextual and parenting factors that might mediate these associations. In addition, it is hard to interpret findings based on global parent reports of screen time alone because, as mentioned earlier, parents have wide-ranging motivations for using digital media with and around their young children. For example, associations between children's digital media use and their attention development may be bidirectional, with parents using digital media as a tool to regulate children with worse attention and inhibitory control skills (Cliff et al., 2018).

To the extent that digital media use disrupts executive function and attention, digital media use may have broader implications for cognitive development in general. For examples, Lin et al. (2015) found a higher frequency of cognitive delay in a high-television exposure group compared to a matched low-television exposure group in 2-year-olds; Tomopoulos et al. (2010) found a longitudinal negative relation between television exposure at 6 months and cognitive development 1 year later; and Zhang et al. (2022) found a difference in working memory capacity, with higher performance among 3- to 5-year-olds who adhered to screen time recommendations performing better than 3- to 5-year-olds who did not.

2.5.4 Social Competence

Socioemotional skills, including a child's ability to read and respond to social cues, recognize and regulate emotional states, and adapt to external challenges, have also been linked to early digital media use. Longitudinal studies have demonstrated that early television viewing, and especially viewing adult-directed or violent content, is associated with worse emotion and attention regulation (Gueron-Sela & Gordon-Hacker, 2020; Hinkley et al., 2014; McDaniel & Radesky, 2018; Zimmerman & Christakis, 2007). For example, in a longitudinal study of 2- to 6-year-olds that controlled baseline levels of emotional and social behaviors, early digital media use was associated with later emotional problems but not social problems (Hinkley et al., 2014). As with other outcomes, disruptions to routines due to digital media use were associated with poorer social emotional outcomes (Raman et al., 2017). Processes are not well understood but have been attributed to a range of factors, including displacement of high-quality social interactions as described elsewhere.

Parents' use of media to escape from stress and parenting or to regulate children's emotions and behavior may be particularly disruptive to infant socio-emotional development (Coyne et al., 2021; McDaniel & Radesky, 2018). Moreover, there is evidence for bidirectional effects, with negative child affect and poor self-regulation predicting media use several months later for both children (Coyne et al., 2021; McDaniel & Radesky, 2020; Neville et al., 2021) and parents (McDaniel & Radesky, 2018). Neville and colleagues (2021) collected data at ages 3, 5, 7, and 9 years and recorded digital media quality and behavioral problems at each time point. They found bidirectional associations between screen time and internalizing problems. However, children's initial levels of externalizing behaviors were associated with later increases in screen time, but not vice versa. McDaniel and Radesky (2020) also observed a pattern of bidirectional associations between media quantity and externalizing behaviors in 1- to 5-year-olds. Cascading effects are shown in longitudinal associations between digital media use, child behavior, and parenting stress (McDaniel & Radesky, 2018, 2020). That is, more media use may increase behavioral problems, but media may also be used to reduce parenting stress or calm a child's difficult behavior resulting in a cascade of increasing screen use and negative child behaviors.

In summary, multiple facets of family media ecology have been studied in isolation. Proposed processes underlying these patterns of results include displacement of uninterrupted sleep and play and changes in parent–child interactional quality, among others. Research in some areas has clearly illustrated the importance of digital media content as a moderator of associations between digital media use and child outcomes. Other areas have begun to focus on contextual factors that could moderate effects. Yet few studies have examined both content and context, and many studies are limited to simple measures of child screen time that do not capture variations in content and context or indirect effects resulting from digital media use by others in the family system. Despite near-universal access and adoption of digital media use during a child's early years (Rideout & Robb, 2020), current theories do not often consider how these facets are interrelated and contribute to the developing child growing up in a digital world. Thus, a new conceptual framework is needed to advance the field of family media ecology.

3 Review of Theoretical Models of Digital Media Effects That Inform the DREAMER Framework

To inform future research on child digital media effects, researchers need a comprehensive theoretical framework that encompasses the complexity of digital media use. Researchers have developed theoretical models to enable predictions about the effects of content and context of media exposure on individual children. Two key elements for conceptualizing the family media ecology include a systems lens that considers bidirectional effects among individuals within the family system and a transactional lens that considers bidirectional effects that unfold over time (e.g., Bornstein, 2009; Bronfenbrenner & Morris, 2006; Sameroff, 2010). Two prominent perspectives incorporate these constructs within the context of child media use: the Differential Susceptibility to Media Effects Model and the Interactional Theory of Childhood Problematic Media Use. Here we briefly summarize these two perspectives, then identify additional considerations that emphasize relational and dynamic perspectives, and finally propose an integrated model designed to capture relational and transactional processes within the family media ecology toward understanding media effects on children.

3.1 The Differential Susceptibility to Media Effects Model

The Differential Susceptibility to Media Effects Model (DSMM; Valkenburg & Peter, 2013; Valkenburg et al., 2021) posits that children are not affected uniformly by digital media exposure; children and families with different characteristics will develop different relations with, and impacts from, the digital media they use. The DSMM model builds on a rich body of research on differential susceptibility in other contexts. Differential susceptibility refers to the idea that some children, due to biological predispositions and social/contextual factors, may be both more vulnerable to negative environmental factors and more likely to benefit from positive environmental factors.

Valkenburg and Peter extended the model explicitly to digital media as a potential and ubiquitous environmental factor that might have differential risks and benefits for children. Specifically, the model posits that child factors (e.g., temperament) and distal contextual factors (e.g., socioeconomic status) contribute to the impact of digital media use on developmental outcomes. The model highlights three types of susceptibility to media: dispositional, developmental, and social. The DSMM has been applied to children and adolescents but can be applied to their parents as well. The model emphasizes media response states and the bidirectional nature of digital media effects, concluding that digital media and the individuals using them are inseparable. Whereas most research on children and digital media treats psychosocial factors as a confounder (e.g., adjusting for family socioeconomic status), the DSMM conceptualizes psychosocial factors of both the child and the parent as intricately interwoven with family digital media use. In addition, the DSMM posits that media effects are bidirectional; for example, just as media use may affect children's self-regulation skills, so too might children's self-regulation skills influence whether and how they use media.

3.1.1 Differential Susceptibility through Child Factors

Children may be differentially susceptible to digital media effects due to factors such as differences in temperament, which can change the probability that media will be used as an emotion regulation technique. Infants with difficult temperament, excessive fussing, or regulatory problems are exposed to more media (Radesky et al., 2014b; Thompson et al., 2013). Parents who report that their children have more difficult temperaments also report that they are more likely to use media to regulate children's emotions (Coyne et al., 2021; Gordon-Hacker & Gueron-Sela, 2020; McDaniel & Radesky, 2018), which may in turn disrupt children's ability to self-regulate as well as the parents' ability to support children as they learn to identify and manage their mood and physiological states. The use of digital media to regulate contributes to a cascade of negative effects as children find it more difficult to regulate, more difficult to transition away from media (Gordon-Hacker & Gueron-Sela, 2020), and more difficult to sleep. Children then experience behavioral problems and parents in turn use more media to regulate children's behavior (Coyne et al., 2021), perpetuating the negative cascade. Conversely, children with easygoing temperaments may not exhibit negative behaviors when asked to transition away from media, even in the context of regulatory use or engagement-prolonging design and may be less likely to develop as many problematic media use habits. Research is needed to assess these possibilities.

3.1.2 Differential Susceptibility through Sociocontextual Factors

According to the DSMM and multiple studies, distal contextual factors moderate digital media effects in several ways. For example, digital media exposure rates and practices differ by ethnicity/race (Calvert et al., 2005). Black and Latine/x parents are more likely than White parents to report discussing media content with their children (Lauricella et al., 2016). Latine/x parents also report greater concern than White or Black parents about the risks of digital media exposure, and they are more likely to report setting rules about media usage (Lauricella et al., 2016; Rideout, 2015). Some digital advertising is disproportionately targeted at families of color, which may impact usage practices (Radesky et al., 2020b).

Digital media access also differs by socioeconomic status (SES: Barr, 2019b). There are disparities in access to quality content and stable internet access by SES (Katz et al., 2019). Most families now own mobile devices, but there are issues of ongoing inequality in the form of inconsistent access to the Internet due to poor bandwidth and reliance on older devices (Katz et al., 2019), suggesting there may be functional differences in media use for families with fewer resources compared with middle- or upper-SES families. Linebarger and colleagues (2014) demonstrated that children from lower-income homes who viewed more educational television content had better attentional and socio-emotional regulation than those from lower-income homes who did not view high levels of educational media content, but this effect was not observed for children from higher-income homes. Relatedly, children from low-SES homes who viewed violent content and who viewed media in the evening were more likely to have a poor quality sleep than children from high-SES homes who had similar media use patterns (Garrison et al., 2011).

The DSMM has been a useful model for examining variation in digital media effects, particularly across individuals. While the DSMM acknowledges digital media use is likely to vary as a function of developmental factors, such as attention skills, much of the research based on the DSMM has focused on school-age children and adolescents, with relatively less emphasis on infancy and early childhood. Moreover, the DSMM places little emphasis on the relational context of digital media use, which is especially important during early development. In addition, the theory acknowledges media content as it relates to individual differences (e.g., selection of media that matches one's interests) but pays less attention to novel design affordances of newer media. The model also focuses on distal contextual factors (e.g., SES) with less attention to proximal contexts (e.g., parent motivations for using digital media, indirect effects of parents' own media use). Filling some of these gaps, the Interactional Theory of Childhood Problematic Media Use has overlapping dimensions with the DSMM while additionally focusing on proximal contexts and the ways in which digital design maintains child engagement with media.

3.2 The Interactional Theory of Childhood Problematic Media Use

Drawing from Bronfenbrenner and Morris's PPCT model (2006), the Interactional Theory of Childhood Problematic Media Use (IT-CPU; Domoff et al., 2020) focuses on problematic media use, such as sneaking or lying about media, a preoccupation with media, difficulty stopping engaging in media, using media as a coping mechanism, increased media-related conflict in the family, increased desire to spend time on media, and significant frustrations when access to digital media is denied. The IT-CPU posits that three primary components may impact childhood problematic media use (PMU): distal factors (context of the environment or situation, such as the parent–child relationship), proximal factors (antecedents to problematic media use), and maintaining factors (processes that reinforce problematic media use).

Research has begun to use the IT-CPU to examine how these factors are related to the emergence of PMU over time. Proximal processes involve direct antecedents to developing PMU. For example, a highly reactive child temperament tends to be related to higher levels of PMU during early childhood (Coyne et al., 2021). Additionally, parental media monitoring (specifically rule setting) when children are 2 years old appears to be protective for the development of PMU over time by 4 years of age (Coyne et al., 2023c; Shawcroft et al., 2023). Viewing educational media content tends to be related to lower levels of PMU over time (compared to non-educational or violent media) (Coyne et al., 2022c). In other words, child characteristics, parental practices around media, or overt features of media content are directly related to the development of PMU. More research needs to address precursors and trajectories of PMU in order to develop prevention and intervention strategies.

Distal factors refer to the general environment that may have a more indirect impact on the development of PMU during childhood. For example, parental depression (Holmgren et al., 2022), parental exhaustion, and parental harsh criticism directed toward the child are all associated with PMU (Swit et al., 2023). Conversely, general parental efficacy tends to be protective against PMU over time (Coyne et al., 2023). These constructs are not directly related to child digital media use but may provide an environment where child PMU is likely to blossom. For example, parents with greater parenting efficacy may provide alternative activities for children, whereas children of parents with harsh or controlling parenting style may use media to avoid family activities.

Finally, maintaining factors are processes that reinforce PMU over time. These are studied less than proximal or distal factors, although they are important for understanding the reasons why PMU persists over time. Maintaining factors might take the form of media design features intended to keep children engaged and coming back to digital media devices. Additionally, maintaining factors might include the use of media to regulate emotions, where children learn to rely on media for coping and mood management (Coyne et al., 2022b).

This theory takes a more comprehensive lens to the study of PMU as a child outcome and highlights the importance of studying the overall family ecology (both media and non-media related) to understand the development of PMU. However, the IT-CPU is only focused on one child media use outcome (i.e., PMU) and does not extend to other types of child digital media engagement or developmental outcomes.

3.3 Other Perspectives with Implications for Digital Media Effects

The two foregoing models provide a foundation to study child digital media use from a wider ecological lens. However, these two models do not include other critical factors. Next, we describe research and theory that draw on several concepts (media motivations; family systems and dynamics; developmental cascades; cognitive constraints; and human–computer actions) that are not specifically addressed by DSMM or IT-CPU, and then offer a new conceptual approach to media research that integrates new concepts with existing models.

3.3.1 Parent Motivations for Digital Media Use

Some theories focus on the drivers of parent and child digital media use. For example, the Uses and Gratifications framework (Rubin, 1986) posits that decisions to use media at all, and to select certain types of media, vary based on momentary needs and wants. While initially created to characterize adults' own digital media use, it has been extended (albeit sparingly) to characterize parents' decisions about their child's digital media use. The IT-CPU focuses specifically on parents' use of media to regulate their child's emotional and behavioral states, but there are many other reasons that parents may use (or not use) media with and around their young children. For example, Nikken (2019) observed that parents report allowing child media use to meet a wide range of parents' needs, such as occupying children so the parent can get things done. Other reasons for media use include (but are not limited to) escaping from stress and conflict, educating children, and bonding through shared media use. The causes and consequences are parents' motivations to use (or not use) digital media with and around their young children are best understood through a family systems perspective, to which we turn next.

3.3.2 Family Systems Perspective

Family systems theory posits that interactions between different family members represent an open and ongoing system that may be influenced by the environment (in this case, digital media; Brockerick, 1993; Galvin et al., 2006). When individuals within the family system interact with one another, change and growth occur over time. Additionally, these patterns of interactions are shaped by external forces, such as digital media. This might play out in multiple ways (e.g., Padilla-Walker et al., 2012). For example, a positive and warm relationship between parent and child might impact the child's relationship with digital media, perhaps posting family events, choosing to interact with family members, and so on. Alternatively, the child's relationship with digital media might impact the relationship between their parents. Perhaps the child is overusing media and shows problematic use and parents are arguing over best parenting practices. In other words, different systems within the family unit and around digital media shape the way those in the family interact over the course of development. In this way, a family systems approach can encompass relational factors (e.g., technoference, joint media engagement) that have been largely overlooked by other theoretical models.

Given that parents are often gatekeepers of young children's media use, a complete understanding of the causes and consequences of media use requires one to consider family processes that lead to digital media use. Such processes are an integral part of the family media ecology and can be understood through a family systems lens. For example, some scholars have posited that strict prohibitions on children's digital media use can be a risk factor for parental burnout (Mikolajczak & Roskam, 2018). Such a framing implies that parents use digital media as resources to promote parents' own well-being, which could have positive downstream effects for children. Such a family systems lens would consider not only the direct effects of digital media use on the child but also indirect effects via parents' mental health and wellbeing. We posit that the degree to which media use represents a risk versus a resource depends on several factors, including the reasons parents choose media (e.g., to take a break for themselves), the way media are used (e.g., solitary versus joint media engagement), and the way media use is experienced (e.g., as a source of parenting support/advice versus shame/doubt; as a constant distraction versus a much-needed respite). In this way, research on the causes and consequences of media use can consider the impact on multiple family members; what might be an opportunity cost for one family member (e.g., displacing opportunities for high-quality parent–child interaction) may be a resource for another family member (e.g., providing a moment to destress instead of lashing out; Torres et al., 2021).

3.3.3 Relational Dynamics and Developmental Cascades

Child development is nested within early relationships with caregivers and siblings that shape each other over time (Sameroff, 2010). In addition, development across different domains is dynamic, and development in one domain affects development in another in the form of developmental cascades. These cascades result in both immediate changes in responses and cumulative long-term changes in child outcomes (Tamis-LeMonda, 2021). For example, when infants' gradually transition from crawling to walking, they are able to explore objects in different ways which also elicits different verbal responses from others around them (Karasik et al., 2016). A relational dynamics perspective recognizes that interactions among individuals and the environment are variable across short timescales. For example, in addition to large-scale developmental changes over time, one's emotional and behavioral states vary moment to moment and day to day. Family members may feel more exhausted or more connected on some days than others.

Many theoretical approaches aimed at understanding digital media effects have an implicit assumption that effects are static, manifesting as between-person differences, although there are some exceptions (e.g., arousal response states characterized by the DSMM). Although the DSMM recognizes the transactional nature of children's media use and preferences, it does not explicitly examine the relational processes that occur around media (e.g., parent–child interaction around tablets; Munzer et al., 2019), or are disrupted or supported by media (e.g., technoference; McDaniel & Coyne, 2016). Furthermore, the interplay between caregiver media use, child media use, and relational concepts such as attachment, co-regulation, and mentalization (i.e., caregiver mental models of their child; Rosenblum et al., 2002) are not addressed by DSMM. For example, child regulatory uses of media are inherently a dyadic process in which a caregiver interprets a child's emotional state, experiences their own emotional reaction that drives a co-regulation or media-regulation behavior, and experiences relief when the child's affect is subsequently regulated. Although IT-CPU includes parenting style, parent–child relationship quality, and proximal parent–child interaction factors as drivers and maintainers of PMU, it does not consider how these factors shape each other over time, through micro-cascades in daily interactions or macro-cascades over different developmental windows. Furthermore, while IT-CPU's narrow focus on PMU allows for examination of a clinically related outcome, a broader lens on social, emotional, language, cognitive, sleep, parent well-being, and other health and developmental domains is needed. A comprehensive theoretical framework would also allow for testing digital media effects both between and within individuals and across multiple timescales.

3.3.4 Cognitive Constraints and Developmental Considerations

Several researchers have focused on cognitive constraints and how they directly influence learning from digital media (e.g., Barr & Kirkorian, 2023; Fisch, 2000, 2017; Hipp et al., 2017). Learning from digital media is cognitively challenging for children under 4 years of age because the images are presented in two dimensions and have to be related to objects in the three-dimensional world. Additionally, digital media often violate the physical constraints of the real world (e.g., abrupt jumps in time and space) and may incorporate fantastical or unfamiliar content. Learning from media therefore places a high degree of cognitive load on the child.

During early childhood, at least until the age of 4 years, children typically experience a transfer deficit, learning approximately 50% less from media presentations than from face-to-face interactions (Barr, 2013; Strouse & Samson, 2021). Several processes have been proposed to explain the transfer deficit. Media are perceptually impoverished and contain fewer cues compared to real-life presentations (e.g., Barr & Hayn, 1999). There are also fewer social and interactional cues available in media (e.g., Hipp et al., 2017). Additionally, there are information processing constraints on learning. Until about 3 years old, children are less likely to remember information when cues at encoding do not match cues at retrieval, for example, when the color of the object is different in one situation than another. The ability to remember information in the face of such perceptual changes has been termed representational flexibility (Barr, 2013, 2019). Additionally, these young children do not fully understand that one object can represent or stand in for another object, which is termed a lack of symbolic understanding (Troseth, 2010; Troseth et al., 2019). For example, children under 3 years of age may not understand that the screen is an object in itself and that actions shown on a screen can stand for or symbolize actions out in the real world. All of these cognitive constraints likely contribute to a transfer deficit in young children.

By 4 years of age, the transfer deficit typically declines, likely due to increased experience with media as well as the acquisition of age-related cognitive skills such as working memory and inhibitory control (Barr & Kirkorian, 2023; Hipp et al., 2017; Kirkorian, 2018). Once children overcome the transfer deficit, the extent to which they learn from media continues to depend on both children's own characteristics (e.g., prior knowledge, working memory capacity) and the degree to which media content is designed in ways that increase or decrease cognitive load (Barr & Kirkorian, 2023; Fisch, 2000, 2017). The Science of Learning pillars of learning (Pillar 1: Active Learning, Pillar 2: Engagement in the Learning Process, Pillar 3: Meaningful Learning, Pillar 4: Social Interaction, see Table 1) have been applied to media content as quality indicators (Hirsh-Pasek et al., 2015). As described earlier, content analyses applying these learning pillars have found the quality of educational apps is typically poor (Meyer et al., 2021). However, a well-designed educational content will increase the likelihood of transfer of learning (Fisch, 2017; Wright et al., 2001).

Taken together, cognitive constraints on information processing, combined with media design, will result in different levels of cognitive load for individual children at different points in development (Barr & Kikorian, 2023; Hipp et al., 2017). These constraints on processing need to be considered when determining media effects, including the degree to which educational media content may produce positive outcomes or buffer against negative outcomes of media use.

3.3.5 The Role of Human–Computer Interactions

Modern digital media (e.g., mobile devices, touchscreen apps, immersive video games, personalized video-sharing sites, video streaming services) have novel design affordances that require updated conceptual frameworks and measurement approaches compared to traditional media. With the introduction of smartphones in 2007 and tablets in 2010, children and parents could take a range of different media types (e.g., video, games, email, messaging) everywhere and use them at all times of day. Mobile devices can be taken into bedrooms, used during mealtimes and bedtime routines, and brought to other settings such as parks and outdoor play spaces. Handheld size and faster Internet speeds and computing power have led to family media ecologies in which digital devices are interwoven into daily life, used on-demand, and are gathering data about users to shape advertising and content delivery. Interactive touchscreen interfaces have also revolutionized how young children engage with and learn from media content, with potential for interactive scaffolds overcoming cognitive constraints or audiovisual enhancements causing distraction and cognitive overload.

Research on how design affordances interact with user psychology – the field of Human–Computer Interaction (HCI) – demonstrates that subtle changes in interactive design can shape human behavior in meaningful ways. For example, designs that constrain user choice, create a false sense of urgency, or prompt the user to return to technology frequently to meet the technology developer's business interests of data collection or advertising impressions – at the expense of the user's interests (i.e., time, money, sleep) – have been termed "dark patterns." These manipulative design patterns have been documented as widespread in video games (Gray et al., 2018), e-commerce websites (Mathur et al., 2019), and children's apps (Radesky et al., 2022), but no studies have examined how they influence family well-being. Other relevant design affordances include engagement-prolonging designs that use variable rewards, low-friction (e.g., autoplay next episode), and high-pleasure content (e.g., infinite scroll with satisfying content) that extend children's and caregivers' time online at the expense of higher-friction play or relational activities.

HCI-related concepts relevant to parenting have been explored in interviews with parents, who described feeling "hooked" by their device's rewards and notifications, overloaded by the amount of information available, and conflicted about whether to respond to child needs versus "escape" into a satisfying experience of social media (Radesky et al., 2016c). Similarly, analysis of children's YouTube viewing habits suggests that the majority of children's time spent on this platform includes low-quality user-generated content featuring commercial products attractive to children (e.g., candy, toys; Radesky et al., 2020c). In contrast, human-centered or child-centered design has interactive features that support the goals and agency of the user, allowing discovery of positive content as well as disengagement (Radesky & Hiniker, 2022).

Once design affordances and HCI concepts are emphasized in child development research, the importance of individual differences becomes more evident. Engagement-promoting features interact persuasively with users' unique attentional, emotional, and social characteristics (Fogg, 2009). First, children and parents have differential responses to interactive design nudges based on characteristics such as executive functioning, visual processing, or emotional reactivity. Children with weaker impulse inhibition may be more susceptible to following engagement-prolonging designs such as autoplay or in-game rewards. Parents with higher emotional reactivity might find the frictionless digital environment of social media more reinforcing when using media as a "virtual escape" in the setting of parent–child conflict. Furthermore, parent and child characteristics are inferred and profiled through their use of digital platforms such as social media, mobile games, and video-sharing services, which shapes what content they are recommended. Therefore, to understand how HCI processes drive or maintain media use behaviors it is important to characterize both the user's strengths and weaknesses as well as the design affordances of media that they use most.

4 Developing a New Conceptual Framework for Understanding Digital Media Effects on Children: The DREAMER Framework

Each of these theoretical perspectives captures important dimensions of early digital media exposure and developmental trajectories. However, they can work together for a unified developmental and family systems approach. Such an approach would consider relational and emotional dynamics as well as the cognitive constraints and design features that moderate media effects. An updated framework needs to consider the role of multiple factors broadly construed as content and context. Such a framework would consider how families may be able to harness digital media as a resource to meet multiple needs. Theoretical models often ignore early sensitive developmental windows where media use patterns may be established and maintained. Digital media use can be a solo or shared experience and developmental outcomes are reliant on those parameters, particularly early in development. We propose a new conceptual framework rather than an all-encompassing theoretical model, with a focus on dynamic and relational factors that are particularly important during infancy and early childhood. We suggest that each component requires systematic research to understand the underlying processes and to better inform interventions.

We propose the Dynamic, Relational, Ecological Approach to Media Effects Research (DREAMER) framework that incorporates elements of family systems and relational theory drawing on Bronfenbrenner and Morris's (2006) ecological model and Sameroff's (2010) transactional and dialectical model. Whereas Bronfenbrenner conceptualized media at the macro level (level of society) as something that would indirectly influence child outcomes, we reconceptualize media as a proximal context that directly and frequently influences the parent–child microsystem. Similarly, focusing on adolescent development, Navarro & Tudge (2022) proposed the neo ecological theory as a revised Bronfenbrenner framework, adding technology to the microsystem and theorizing that there are both physical and virtual microsystems in which adolescents engage. We argue that the virtual microsystem is also critical for parents.

The DREAMER framework considers the fact that children's digital media are continuously and rapidly evolving and include increasingly sophisticated ways of providing targeted individualized content to children. Adding a relational and family systems approach to existing theories will help anticipate and address issues posed by new technologies as they arise. Our conceptual framework also draws on the DSMM (Valkenburg & Peter, 2013), IT-CPU (Domoff et al., 2020), and Uses and Gratifications (Rubin, 1986) to understand the causes and consequences of media use in the family context. We expand on these models by including momentary as well as cumulative effects over time. We include elements of the IT-CPU model to recognize the role of the wider family ecology and both the content and context of media on child problematic media use. We extend the IT-CPU model to examine all types of media use (not just problematic patterns) and link media use to more child developmental outcomes. We maintain the core transactional nature of DSMM considering how individual child characteristics and characteristics of the family media ecology interact across time and cumulatively predict long-term outcomes. We extend the DSMM by considering in-the-moment interactions and parental motivation for media use (or lack thereof). We incorporate the Uses and Gratification framework, conceptualizing media use as an active process designed to meet different parent needs (e.g., to take a break from parenting or regulate their child's behavior). We extend the Uses and Gratifications framework by conceptualizing family members' digital media use as a resource for parents that can be reflected in intra-individual variation over time.

We also build upon each of the existing theories by considering the entire family media ecology. That is, the DREAMER framework considers the reciprocal effects of digital media use among children and adults in a family system. In this way, the DREAMER framework is designed to capture both direct effects of digital media use on children and indirect effects that reflect family processes (e.g., technoference reducing parent–child interactions versus joint media engagement increasing parent–child interactions). Within the DREAMER framework, some uses of media may meet parents' needs in supportive ways, but using media to regulate children's emotions and behavior may be problematic for children's self-regulation development (Coyne et al., 2021; McDaniel & Radesky, 2018). Motivations for media restriction are also considered (e.g., parents' desire to protect children from harmful media content). We also consider the use of media content in each of these contexts, and how parent and child characteristics predict in-the-moment decisions regarding content choices for both parents and children. Finally, responses to media are also considered in light of design affordances that may prolong engagement with media, and guide future decisions about media use motivations.

Overall, the framework considers the dynamic relational nature of family media ecology. The framework is shown in Figure 1 and includes examples (not exhaustive) of three broad features: individual and contextual factors (individual, relational, and family characteristics, structural factors), media dynamics at varied timescales (media motivations, media use, media responses), and individual and relational outcomes. As shown in Figure 1, the model is dynamic.

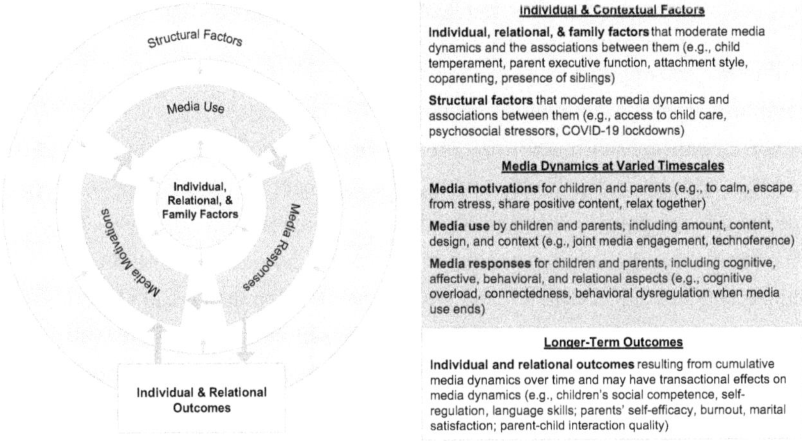

Figure 1 DREAMER Framework and examples for each element of the model.

The middle circle of the figure shows how parents' motivations for using (or not using) media predict media use and then media responses in the moment, which then predicts parents' motivations for using (or not using) media in future moments. Although researchers have considered the role of temperament as a child moderator, particularly as it pertains to differential susceptibility in the DSMM, they have not focused on social competence and emotion regulation through a relational lens which we show operating via the dynamic loop as media responses, which expand on the response states conceptualized in the DSMM to include parent responses (e.g., parental stress and burnout) and relational responses (e.g., parent–child interaction quality, connectedness). Individual and structural factors also interact with different components of the model. These levels expand on the developmental, dispositional, and social susceptibility factors in the DSMM by considering the larger family system and relational processes.

Expanding upon prior frameworks (e.g., DSMM, IT-CPU), mechanisms and outcomes in the DREAMER framework are considered at multiple timescales. At shorter timescales, responses to digital media include immediate or short-term outcomes of media use that both predict future media use (i.e., reasons parents do or do not use media) in the short term as well as cumulative effects of media use over time. For example, parental stress and sleep may be immediate responses to media, but cumulatively these patterns will also result in different longer-term outcomes which will in turn influence the short-term relational responses. For example, children's immediate responses to media use (e.g., calming down after a media break versus having a tantrum when media are taken away) may predict the likelihood of parents' using media to calm children at future time points and may mediate longer-term impacts of media use on children's self-regulation and likelihood of a problematic media use profile. Similarly, parents' immediate responses to media use (e.g., feeling relaxed versus cognitively fatigued) may predict the likelihood of parents using media to relax and unwind at future time points and mediate longer-term impacts of media use on parents' mental health (e.g., parental burnout) and children's development (e.g., language acquisition affected by parent–child interactions). In this way, the DREAMER framework expands upon the IT-CPU by considering the entire family media ecology and interaction among different developmental domains. Finally, the DREAMER framework recognizes that parent and child responses to digital media can be interdependent; for instance, whether media use ends in a calmer or more distressed child is likely to affect a parent's momentary stress level and future decisions about whether, when, and how to use digital media.

4.1 Features of the DREAMER Conceptual Framework

4.1.1 Individual, Relational, and Family Characteristics

Our framework includes individual child characteristics, such as child temperament and working memory, that have been associated with media effects. However, we consider that individual child characteristics such as temperament may also moderate how children respond to media. Other individual differences, including neurodiversity and gender development, also need to be considered. Similarly, parent characteristics (e.g., parent executive function), relational characteristics (e.g., child–parent attachment style), and family characteristics (e.g., presence of siblings, family structure, cultural practice) can influence whether and how media are used and how children and parents respond to media.

4.1.2 Structural Factors

The DREAMER framework also considers structural factors that can be associated with media use patterns and effects. For example, there are differences in media use as a function of household income and ethnicity/race. These findings are often descriptive and have not received enough empirical investigation. For example, African American children have higher rates of media exposure than children from other racial and ethnic groups (e.g., Calvert et al., 2005; Hedderson et al., 2023; Kabali et al., 2015). The reasons for this use within families of color with children under 5 are poorly understood, but could include factors such as lower access to child care or recreational centers in historically disinvested communities. In addition, the representation of different races and ethnicities within digital media can be considered both a structural factor (e.g., due to low diversity among writers, animators, actors) and a design affordance factor (e.g., due to platform recommendation of content containing racial/ethnic stereotypes or insufficient removal of white supremacist content that violates platform policies). In each case, existing research using global screen time measures is not explanatory. Structural factors can also moderate media effects. For example, because well-designed educational content has the potential to enhance learning and serve as a resource, educational content has stronger effect sizes for children from low-resourced homes (e.g., Wright et al., 2001). Conversely, low-quality content that includes engagement prolonging strategies is likely to exacerbate negative outcomes, particularly for children who do not have access to other activities (e.g., Linebarger et al., 2014). Other structural factors within low-income homes impact media use. For example, housing density is higher in low-income families, and siblings may share bedrooms and devices which changes media use patterns (e.g., younger siblings observing media content and activities of older siblings). As one example, infants with older siblings watch more child-directed content (Barr et al., 2010). Such dynamic, relational factors within the family have largely been ignored in the literature but can be tested within the DREAMER framework.

4.1.3 Media Motivations

We argue that during early childhood, parents act as gatekeepers of media use in the household and media may be used (or avoided) by both parents and children for multiple purposes. Parents' (including mothers' and fathers') reasons for using and not using media predict media use patterns, such as whether, when, how, and with whom media are used. Such motivations may differ between parents in the same family system. For example, parents may use media to regulate their own emotions (e.g., to calm down when upset) or to regulate their children's emotions and behavior (e.g., to calm them down, to help them fall asleep). If digital media are used to help a child fall asleep, then this family media use practice will determine the timing of media use in the household. Similarly, parents may have reasons for refraining from media use, such as wanting to protect children from harmful media content or preferring to engage in other activities (e.g., reading picture books, playing outdoors). Furthermore, parents use media to calm themselves down, to mentally escape, to relax or to take a break from their children, or to seek social support (Suh et al., 2024; Torres et al., 2021). These parental motivations for media use may result in technoference in the moment, but they may also improve parent–child interactions later on by providing a means for parents to receive support from friends or family. Additional research is needed to investigate how parents' motivations for media impact child behaviors and parent–child relationships.

4.1.4 Media Use Patterns

We argue that media use patterns must be comprehensively measured to capture the quantity, content, design affordances, and proximal context in which digital media are used (e.g., when, with whom). These media use patterns differentially interact with child characteristics and parental factors. For example, if media are used at bedtime, then for children who find it more difficult to fall asleep, engagement-prolonging media may increase arousal and exacerbate sleep onset difficulty. We also argue that different media use patterns may predict different individual (e.g., feeling calm versus aroused) and relational responses (e.g., feeling connected versus distant). Parent use has typically only focused on mothers and not other caregivers in the family media ecology such as fathers, grandparents, and childcare providers. Similarly, most research examines a single focal child, overlooking the interdependence among siblings in households with more than one child.

4.1.5 Responses to Media

Immediate responses to media (e.g., calming down after a media break versus having difficulty transitioning away from media) are analogous to the cognitive, affective, and physiological responses states conceptualized in the DSMM. However, the DREAMER framework expands this conceptualization to add relational and behavioral responses and to represent all individuals in the family system. There may be individual differences in responses to media. For example, some individuals may respond with high arousal to media, whereas others have little to no response to the same content. Such responses can also differ in individuals over time based on different media use patterns. For example, a given child may have more difficulty transitioning away from media rife with engagement-prolonging design features than media without these features. As another example, solitary media use may lead parents to feel less connected with their child, whereas joint media engagement may increase their sense of connection.

4.1.6 Longer-Term Individual and Relational Outcomes

The DREAMER framework illustrates how immediate responses to media use can accumulate over time to produce longer-term outcomes. Such outcomes can also become mediators of future outcomes. For example, an immediate response of heightened arousal may disrupt the amount and quality of sleep. Over time, repeated sleep disruption can worsen cognitive and behavioral outcomes. Similarly, the degree to which media use increases versus decreases parents' stress can have long-term implications for parental burnout. For example, remote work could be a double-edged sword, increasing time for parents but also potentially increasing cognitive load due to balancing work and home demands (Radesky et al., 2016). Finally, the combination of media use patterns by different family members could impact relationships over time. For example, due to decreasing costs of devices, the parent and child often view their own media on separate devices at the same time changing how media are shared (Barr et al., 2020). Like other media effects frameworks, the DREAMER framework can be used to conceptualize potential impacts on a range of child (e.g., language, academic achievement, self-regulation, social competence), parent (e.g., burnout, self-efficacy), and relational outcomes (e.g., parent–child interaction quality) while taking into account the dynamic and relational use of media within the family media ecology.

4.2 The COVID-19 Pandemic: A Case Study Using the DREAMER Framework

By way of illustrating how the DREAMER framework can be leveraged to understand the complexity of media effects, we use it to illustrate what is currently known about the ways in which the COVID-19 pandemic shifted the family media ecology and discuss how this shifting landscape may have impacted both child media use and developmental outcomes. We provide some background information on how the pandemic dramatically changed family experiences and then use the DREAMER framework to illuminate how a family media ecology might interact with child behavior during this time of structural change. Figure 2 depicts the various factors that have been studied at a global level, although no study to date has examined the momentary dynamic processes that are central to the DREAMER framework. For ease of interpretation, the figure depicts only the factors that have been studied, not the associations among them. Therefore, there are no arrows in this figure.

The COVID-19 pandemic upended lives for parents and children, resulting in increased parental burnout, experience of negative emotions like worry and anger, and the need to provide care, comfort, and reassurance to their children (Bornstein, 2021; Kerr et al., 2021b). In turn, parents' perceived impact included higher parental burnout, higher child stress, and fewer positive child behaviors (Bornstein, 2021; Kerr et al., 2021a). Related, the pandemic provided an unprecedented media landscape for parents, which, depending on occupation, may

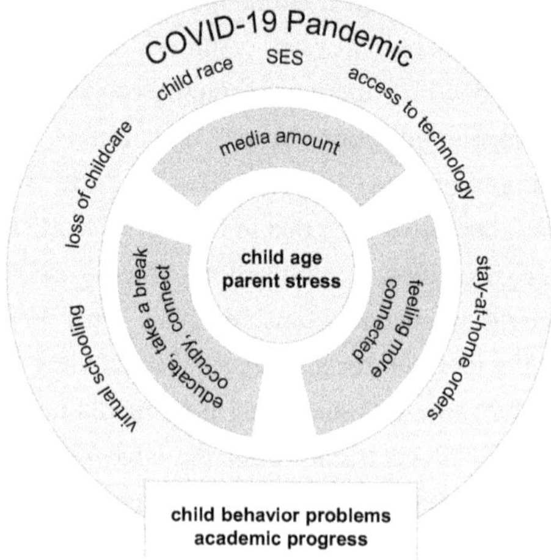

Figure 2 Sample of global (not dynamic/momentary) factors that have been studied in the context of the COVID-19 pandemic, depicted within the DREAMER framework. Note, we do not include any arrows within this graphic because, although different research groups examined how structural and parent and child characteristics were related to media use amount, they did not capture relational and dynamic components of the framework.

have included working from home via videoconferencing and providing coworkers a new glimpse into each others' home lives. In addition, parents were also responding to a global threat which resulted in changes to their own media use patterns, with an increase in checking of news, using social media to provide support to their community, and navigating health-related misinformation. Based on **parental individual characteristics**, digital media use may have come to encompass much of their day, which in turn shaped their availability for parent–child activities and children's own media use.

Research has emerged that examines the interaction of media use and socioemotional development in the context of the COVID-19 pandemic. Across many countries, most families showed little compliance with the American Academy of Pediatrics and other pediatric guidelines regarding children's screen time (Ribner et al., 2021), despite having previously demonstrated some adherence and acknowledgement of those guidelines. These findings provide a window on how the family media ecology shifted in response to increasing demands on the family. Moreover, the COVID-19 pandemic exacerbated preexisting stressors on families and highlighted the reliance on media use in the family context, underscoring the potential risks and benefits of media usage patterns. These preexisting and pandemic-induced stressors experienced by families represent the **parent and child individual characteristics** section of the model.

Perhaps as a coping mechanism to address reduced resources and increased stressors, across multiple countries during lockdown periods, young children's screen media use sharply increased during the pandemic (Bergmann et al., 2022; Carroll et al., 2020; Eales et al., 2021; Gueron-Sela et al., 2023; Hartshorne et al., 2021; Ozturk Eyimaya & Yalçin Irmak, 2021; Pedrotti et al., 2022; Pombo et al., 2021; Ribner et al., 2021; Wiederhold, 2020). Increased use of media during lockdown reflects how **structural factors** (i.e., the pandemic; accessibility of community activities) can influence the **amount of media use** in the DREAMER framework. The increase in media use can depend on **individual child characteristics** (e.g., child age, temperament), **individual parent factors** (e.g., needing to work in the community vs. remotely, stress level, social support), and **structural factors** (e.g., ethnic disparities in access to in-person schooling, and access to technology through remote learning), all of which themselves influence parent and child **outcomes** (e.g., emotional wellbeing; connection to extended family). For example, in a 2020 report focused on children under the age of 6 years living in Canada, parents reported an 87% increase in children's screen time particularly for entertainment (Carroll et al., 2020). In an international study of ~2,500 parents of 3- to 7-year-olds in 6 countries, parents reported a change in media content with an average 40-minute increase in entertainment and a 20-minute increase in educational app use in early 2020 at the beginning of the pandemic (Ribner et al., 2021). The greatest change in usage occurred on weekdays when media use increased to levels more consistently reported during weekends.

Much research during the pandemic focused on **structural factors** and **individual child characteristics** and how they were associated with **media use**, including both increased screen time in general and increased problematic use patterns. Families from lower SES reported higher media use during the pandemic (Ribner et al., 2021). Consistent with prior work showing higher media usage by Black and Latinx children prior to the pandemic (Rideout & Robb, 2020), in a study of parents of 4- to 12-year-olds that measured pre- and post-COVID-19 media use, Black and Latinx children had larger overall increases in screen time relative to pre-pandemic levels compared to White children (Hedderson et al., 2023). In a cross-sectional study of parents of 2- to 12-year-olds collected in 2019 and 2020, reports of problematic media use in children over 5 years was higher in 2020 than in 2019 (Eales et al., 2021), suggesting that the age of the child should be considered. Another study conducted in Brazil that compared digital media use in a sample of children under 3 years measured before the COVID-19 pandemic with a sample measured during the COVID-19 pandemic found that media use duration was higher during the pandemic, but only among children over 12 months of age (Pedrotti et al., 2022; see also Hedderson et al., 2023). A study of parents of 4- to 12-year-olds that measured pre- and post-COVID media use also showed that levels of media use, including educational media use, remained elevated post-pandemic after many health restrictions were lifted (Hedderson et al., 2023, see also Gueron-Sela et al., 2023).

Prior studies had also demonstrated stable patterns of media usage within families. Ribner and colleagues (2021) found that parents who reported higher media use before the pandemic also reported higher use during the pandemic showing stability in family media use patterns. All families showed increased usage, but the authors argued that those starting at higher baseline may also find it harder to return to pre-pandemic levels and that individual differences in family media ecology rather than the COVID-19 disruption may be more predictive of future outcomes. This is an open empirical question.

Other researchers focused on **motivations** for the changing media landscape, while taking **structural factors** and **individual child characteristics** into account. For example, instrumental factors likely contributed to these rapid changes in media use, such as meeting immediate educational and childcare needs, to sustain social interactions and to enable parents to work and cope with the multiple stressors that arose during a period of uncertainty (Ribner et al., 2021; Wiederhold, 2020).

Virtual schooling highlighted the digital divide (i.e., **a structural factor**) between rural and urban communities and between wealthy and poor families, with underconnectivity dramatically disrupting academic progress (Katz et al., 2021; Sen & Tucker, 2021). In contrast, when connectivity was available, children experienced benefits not only for ongoing education, but also evidenced by the ability to stay connected to remote family members, particularly grandparents (Strouse et al., 2021; Roche et al., 2022). These findings suggest that access to stable high-speed Internet provided a benefit to family well-being, maintaining multigenerational links with frequent video chat contact during the pandemic. Change in media use as a function of SES may also be resource dependent. Perhaps because high-income workers were more likely at home and lower-income workers were more likely to be essential workers, greater demands on childcare were placed on lower-SES households and digital media were used to cope with those changes (Ribner et al., 2021). Variation in access to video chat highlights the links between **structural factors** (i.e., tech availability and SES), **motivations** (i.e., use of media to connect), and family **outcomes** (i.e., increased connection and reduced stress).

Other research during the pandemic focused on the changes in **media use and design affordances** related to **structural factors** (e.g., virtual schooling) that shifted media use during the pandemic. For example, Eales et al. (2021) used a mixed methods approach, revealing that parents found it more difficult to both monitor media usage and to implement family media rules early in the pandemic when school-aged children had higher access to devices, which provided frictionless access to platforms like YouTube and online games. They also found that media management was easier when parents had fewer children, when both parents were not working full-time, and when the weather was better (i.e., not during winter) – all **structural factors** influencing media use. Parents did not report guilt over media usage during the pandemic, even though they reported that they often felt guilt prior to the pandemic, suggesting that parents were responding to an immediate change in circumstances and resources that influenced their **motivations** for using or not using media and their **responses** to their child's media use. Taken together these findings suggest that increased use of media was a response to a sudden change in availability of resources.

In a longitudinal study, Gueron-Sela and colleagues (2023) tracked families' media use patterns in 2020 during four periods of national lockdown and during a post-lockdown period in Israel. They examined associations between different aspects of media use and post-lockdown behavioral adjustment in a sample of parents of 2- to 5-year-olds. Pre-COVID estimates of media use were retrospectively obtained. Child overall screen time use, exposure to background television, use of media to regulate child distress, and maternal mobile device use all fluctuated throughout the lockdown periods. Moreover, during lockdowns children's behavior problems were concurrently and positively correlated with screen time, use of media to regulate child distress, and exposure to background television. Child media use increased from pre-pandemic to the lockdown and increased even further during the post-lockdown period. However, the key finding was that media use patterns during lockdown were not longitudinally related to child behavior problems in the post-lockdown period. Although this is only one study, the findings suggest that for most children the change in child behavior was likely to be a result of the structural changes surrounding them rather than simply a change in media use and that behaviors are likely to resolve with a return to more typical structure. Together, findings from this study suggest the pandemic (a **structural factor**) affected parent **motivations** (to regulate child distress) and both parent and child **media use** (increased quantity), but did not predict child behavior problems (a **child outcome**) longitudinally.

In summary, changes in media use as a response to the COVID-19 pandemic provide lessons learned regarding family media ecology. One such lesson is that when resources to parents, such as childcare, were reduced, there was an increase in the use of screen media by families across the globe, suggesting that changes in media practices may have been driven by necessity and new motivations for media use (Hartshorne et al., 2021). Virtual schooling highlighted the digital divide between rural and urban communities and between wealthy and poor families, with underconnectivity dramatically disrupting academic progress (Katz et al., 2021; Sen & Tucker, 2021). Some children who did have access to school devices were provided a portal to engagement-prolonging, monetized platforms like YouTube that recommend low-quality and negative content, whereas other school regions placed heavy restrictions on access to content. Moreover, the COVID-19 pandemic exacerbated preexisting economic and psychosocial stressors on families (Bornstein, 2021; Kerr et al., 2021b) and highlighted reliance on media use in the family context, underscoring the potential risks and benefits of media usage patterns (Hedderson et al., 2023; Ribner et al., 2021). Under conditions of heightened stress and unpredictability, media use shifted with demands on parental resources, and compliance with AAP and other pediatric guidelines across different countries was low (Ribner et al., 2021). The changes in media use patterns during the COVID-19 pandemic provide additional insight into why more constant contextual factors, such as low socioeconomic resources and higher parental stress, are consistently associated with higher use of media within households. That is, the **motivations** for media use may represent a coping mechanism to provide additional resources in the form of educational content and entertainment to both parents and their children and potentially reduce stress.

Research on parent and child digital media use during the COVID-19 pandemic provides a useful case study for illustrating the DREAMER framework, with two notable exceptions: First, most studies to date do not adopt a relational lens that considers the interdependence of digital media use and effects among family members. Second, all of the studies described here rely on global estimates of media use and parent and child characteristics (e.g., child distress, behavioral problems). Most studies report findings from cross-sectional analyses, with a comparatively small number reporting longitudinal associations across relatively long time scales. Examining short-term, within-person changes in family members' emotional and behavioral states, particularly as they relate to day-to-day fluctuations in digital media motivations and use, may reveal new patterns of use and entry points for intervention to support parents in their family media practices. If research continues to overlook the real-time family processes that contribute to the family media ecology, interventions aimed at modifying media use may fail to help families, or even do more harm than good by removing one of the few coping mechanisms readily accessible to parents (Wolfers & Schneider, 2020). These changes in family media ecology undoubtedly altered how family members interacted with each other around media. These dynamic and relational changes have not been fully captured in the existing literature. When interpreting future research, the DREAMER framework could be used to consider dynamic and relational complexity within family media ecology.

5 An Evolving Digital Media Landscape: The Problem of Measurement and Content Analysis

Although some theoretical models have begun to capture the complexity of media use and effects, many studies fail to capture this complexity. Conclusions from the extant literature are constrained by imprecise measures of media use, often relying on retrospective parental global estimates of a typical day of the week that fail to capture the complexity of children's and parents' lived experience (e.g., Barr, 2019a, 2019b; Barr et al., 2020). For instance, reexamination of studies in Kostyrka-Allchorne et al.'s (2017) review of media and early cognitive development reveals that most (62%) were based on a single global estimate of typical media use. Critically, only 10% of studies considered family contextual factors (e.g., socioeconomic status, parent co-viewing) as potential moderators of media effects (Barr et al., 2020). All studies were based on a single, self-report measure to examine between-person differences; none captured within-person day-to-day variation. Even when content or context was considered, relying on measures that assume all media use is created equal or that digital media only displace educational and social opportunities results in research that focuses almost exclusively on potentially harmful effects of media (e.g., Barr, 2019a, 2019b; Zimmerman & Christakis, 2009).

Compounding the measurement problem is the fact that the digital world changes daily, and more efficient mechanisms are needed to code the vast amount of content children use. Content contains more artificial intelligence that is highly personalized to the individual user. Progress in understanding the effects of media exposure on child outcomes has been limited by the lack of large and representative longitudinal datasets, the difficulty of tracking the quality of content in an ever-changing media environment, and failure to capture the context in which family members use media for multiple purposes.

Poor measurement represents a substantial gap in the literature, given that both the content and context of media exposure are associated with outcomes during early childhood (Barr & Linebarger, 2017). Furthermore, when more reliable measures of media exposure are used, they are typically not integrated with other comprehensive measures of family life in a systematic way. Time diaries are a particularly robust method for capturing actual media time, content, and context, and diaries have shown high convergence with directly observed media use in homes (Anderson et al., 1985; Barr et al., 2010b; Vandewater & Lee, 2009); however, due to high participant burden on pencil-and-paper diaries, time use diaries are underutilized. Mobile device passive sensing is an unobtrusive, objective measure that is far more accurate than parent report (Barr et al., 2020; Radesky et al., 2020a), but research harnessing passive sensing apps is still in its infancy. New tools and methodologies are needed to capture the complexity of digital media use. Next we describe one approach that leverages multiple complementary measurement tools aimed at characterizing the family media ecology.

5.1 The Comprehensive Assessment of Family Media Exposure (CAFE) Toolkit

In response to limitations in measurement and to capture many factors represented in the DREAMER framework, the Comprehensive Assessment of Family Media Exposure (CAFE) Consortium developed a multi-method, scalable, cost-effective CAFE Toolkit to capture both the quantity and the content and context of media use (Barr et al., 2020). Here we describe the CAFE Toolkit as one example that can be utilized by media researchers interested in studying the causes and consequences of media use in early childhood (see Kirkorian & Barr, 2021 for documentation). It is not meant to be prescriptive. The original CAFE Toolkit measures household media use through a questionnaire, time-use diary, and passive-sensing app installed on family mobile devices (Barr et al., 2020; Radesky et al., 2020b). More recently, the CAFE Toolkit has been expanded to include momentary and daily sampling. All measures can be collected remotely and completed on mobile devices. Each measure is described in more detail later in this section.

The CAFE Toolkit (see Figure 3) considers the entire household, including intentional exposure to child-directed content, unintended child exposure to background media sources, and parent use of media. It captures both supportive, child-centered content and joint media engagement, as well as engagement-prolonging, exploitative media and technoference. The CAFE Consortium members, representing an interdisciplinary and international group of investigators, co-developed the Toolkit. Their use of the Toolkit across studies, ages, and different countries allows for direct comparisons between populations while also allowing for synergistic research where each research group answers specific research questions within their own data set at the same time contributing to a larger, shared, integrated data set for secondary data use.

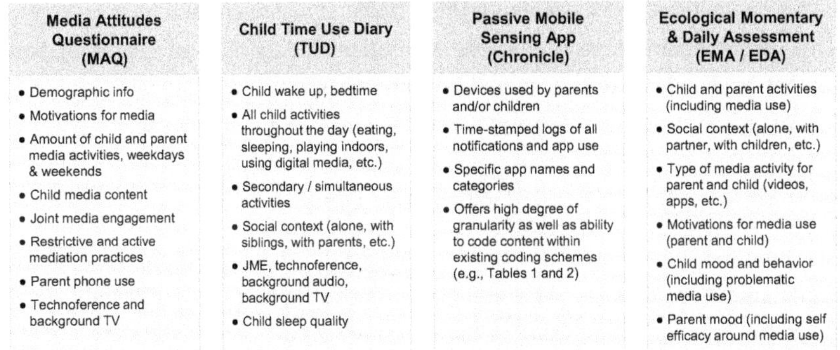

Figure 3 The components of the CAFE Toolkit.

Notably, comprehensive measures such as those in the CAFE Toolkit are burdensome, and it is incumbent on researchers to validate and refine measurement scales. A good example of this systematic psychometric approach is the DISRUPT tool (McDaniel, 2021) which is a 4-item measure of parental perceptions of technoference. A similar approach is being taken to develop measures for the CAFE Toolkit (see Suh et al., 2024). Finally, technology is rapidly changing, and it is critical that assessments focus on broad principles (e.g., child-centered design) rather than being device- or technology-centric. A focus on media practices and design will allow measures of family media use to be more easily updated to adapt in ways that capture newer types of media exposure despite changes in the digital media landscape, while focusing on generalizable principles that influence developmental outcomes.

Next, we describe each element of the CAFE Toolkit in turn, emphasizing how each can be leveraged to capture different factors within the DREAMER framework.

5.1.1 Media Attitudes Questionnaire

The Media Attitudes Questionnaire (MAQ) represents global measures of media attitudes, media practices, and individual and structural factors that may affect both parents' and children's media use and responses. It includes questions about structural factors and parent attitudes and behaviors regarding media, which maps on to the structural factors and individual child and parent characteristics sections of the DREAMER framework. There are also questions about the amount, content, and context of media use. Context questions capture a wide range of **motivations** for media use, including instrumental purposes (e.g., occupying the child so the parent can get things done or take a break) and regulatory purposes (e.g., calming down) for both parent and child media use. Other context questions ask about joint media engagement and technoference. This questionnaire is supplemented with other widely used measures of both **parent and child factors**, including parental stress, parental burnout, child language, child sleep, and parent and child problematic media use.

5.1.2 Time Use Diary

The time-use diary is an online survey that logs the child's activities (e.g., sleep, digital media, outdoor play) throughout the entire day as well as overnight sleep. It can be completed first thing in the morning (asking about yesterday's activities) or at night (asking about today's activities). Digital media content and context (**media use** in the model) is captured using specific questions on what the child was watching and with whom. Follow-up questions capture the context of media use including technoference (e.g., presence of background TV or parent mobile device use during play and mealtimes), media content (e.g., target age group, title of program), and joint media engagement (i.e., other people engaging in child media use). A proxy for physical activity can also be calculated from the reported time playing outdoors. Because the time use diary logs the onset and offset of all activities throughout the day, including overnight sleep, it can be synchronized with other time-stamped data streams (e.g., *Chronicle* passive mobile sensing data capturing parents' frequency of checking their mobile device during each child activity throughout the day).

5.1.3 Passive Mobile Sensing with the Chronicle App

Mobile device use is assessed with *Chronicle*, a passive mobile sensing app for iOS and Android devices to provide continuous data on the timing and content of mobile device use. *Chronicle* is installed on mobile devices, including devices owned by the child when available. This method is particularly robust for capturing the harder-to-remember, short bursts of activity associated with mobile device use (Barr et al., 2020; Radesky et al., 2020a). Passive sensing is more accurate than parents' reporting of their own mobile device use (Yuan et al., 2019) and their preschool-age children's smartphone and tablet use (Radesky et al., 2020a). Yuan and colleagues (2019) conducted a study to test the feasibility of passive sensing on the smartphones of parents with young children. They also collected self-reported data from the same parents on their estimation of both the total duration of use and the pickup frequency. Parent self-reported screen use was inaccurate, with most parents underreporting rather than overreporting both duration and pickup frequency. This imprecision is likely due to the handheld nature of mobile device use (i.e., parents may have more difficulty monitoring mobile device use when children are in different rooms) and engagement that is both intermittent and immersive. In addition, data collection with *Chronicle* has provided insight into children's overnight device usage, access to age-inappropriate mobile games, and inequities in access to quality content (Radesky et al., 2020a). Output from the *Chronicle* Android dashboard provides app lists for each user, including the title, time, and duration of each app used during the data collection period and for categories of use (e.g., social media, productivity) for iOS devices. This method provides an objective measure of capturing **media use** for both parents and children. The time-stamped app usage logs can be integrated with other time-stamped data streams (e.g., EMA, time use diaries) to understand parents' and children's device use in naturalistic contexts.

5.1.4 Ecological Momentary and Daily Assessment (EMA and EDA)

Most research relies on parents' global estimates of "typical" media use, disregarding the real-time family dynamics that underlie parent and child emotions and behavior that lead to, and result from, media use. The EMA and EDA approaches permit examination of multiple parts of the model including **media use, motivations, responses,** and **outcomes**, and so represent a particularly useful tool in examining dynamic and relational components of the family media ecology. This method involves an intensive longitudinal design where participants receive multiple EMA surveys each day (usually via text message) about real-time media use, motivations for such use, and responses to it (e.g., family connectedness, child behavior, and parent emotional states). Additionally, participants receive an EDA survey that allows them to reflect on the overall day (for example how typical their child's media use was or how confident they felt in managing their child's media use for the day). The EDA surveys ensure capturing shorter or less frequent behaviors (e.g., video chat, e-books) that may not be captured using EMA alone. Both surveys can also be expanded to capture data relevant to individual studies (e.g., collecting URLs for YouTube videos watched by the child each day to assess content quality). Most existing research on media use during early childhood has used a between-subjects approach, where individuals with high screen use are compared to those with low screen use, for example. Between-person effects reveal differences at the group level but do not allow for individual heterogeneity to exist and likely mask the true development and impact of media within families. Individual heterogeneity and dyadic processes are marked by moment-to-moment and day-to-day fluctuations around media use, which are characterized as within-person effects. The use of EMA and EDA allows for both between and within comparisons, and in so doing emphasizes dynamic and relational aspects of the DREAMER framework across multiple timescales. These surveys can also be synchronized with other time-stamped data streams (e.g., parents' mobile device use in the hour preceding the EMA survey message).

5.1.5 Future Directions: Assessment of Design Affordances

Because the CAFE Toolkit allows assessment of the vast array of mobile, television, and video content that children and caregivers use, through survey, time use diary, and passive sensing methods, an important next step is to classify the quality of this content. The approach to content and design affordance analysis will vary based on the hypotheses of the particular study – for example, the impact of YouTube educational content on language outcomes in a toddler being cared for by Spanish-speaking grandparents; the impact of engagement-prolonging designs on sleep quantity in a child with weaker impulse control in the context of lax parenting; or the impact of negative media ethnic representations on children's social and identity development. Platform algorithms bin children by characteristics to recommend individualized content, that may or may not support child development. While many factors shape identity development, future research on the effects of such algorithms on identity development and other long-term outcomes is necessary. In addition, content and design affordance coding will need to evolve as digital product design evolves (e.g., evaluating trending content; the impact of different algorithmic recommendations). For our current studies, design affordance coding has largely focused on aspects of interactivity that introduce a heightened cognitive load (e.g., disruptive advertising such as pop-up ads; irrelevant hotspots), contribute to extended time on or difficulty transitioning away from media, recommend negative content, or constrain user agency (see Table 2).

6 Future Directions Using the DREAMER Framework

Rapid changes in the media landscape have created an evidence gap regarding child development in the digital world. Scientists and policymakers have also called for more rigorous research on children and modern media to inform both federal regulations regarding child technology products and the guidance provided to parents of young children (e.g., Barr, 2019a, 2022; Markey, 2018; Radesky, 2020b). In this final section, we highlight what we see as critical areas for future research on the causes and consequences of early media use, emphasizing key themes in the DREAMER framework. Research on family media use lends itself to a citizen science approach. Community members can provide insight into data capture methods. In addition, community advisory boards

Table 2 Coding examples of design affordances relevant to the family media ecology.

Category	Description
Distraction: Advertising	Banner ads, pop-up ads, rewards or prompts to watch ad videos
Interactive design	Extraneous interactive hotspots, excessive rewards for completing tasks, gamification, fast pacing, salient features
Engagement promotion	Autoplay, providing "feed" of suggested videos or games for child, rewards for gameplay, navigation constraints
YouTube channels/user-generated content	High level of commercialization, prompts to watch more/subscribe more, low-quality or negative content, long duration with filler

should be solicited to guide researchers about the motivations for media use patterns within families, what questions are most critical for researchers to answer, and how researchers can best communicate research findings.

6.1 Individual Parental Characteristics and Family Media Ecology

Parental and relational family factors are critical parts of family media ecology and require additional empirical attention. There is a wide range of child and parent factors that may influence digital media motivations, use, responses, and effects. For example, parent executive function is known to shape parenting responses (Deater-Deckard et al., 2012), household structure (Deater-Deckard et al., 2014), and parents' own media use (Ophir et al., 2009). Moreover, parent executive function is biologically linked to child executive function development (Coolidge et al., 2000). Therefore, parents with weaker executive function may experience more cognitive load from their media use, have more difficulty multitasking between technology and child demands, and experience greater impact on short-term and longer-term parent–child interaction sensitivity. No prior work has examined the role of parent executive function in digital media and child socioemotional development. Such research could help tailor education and intervention efforts to meet the needs of individual parents.

We also know little about daily fluctuations in parents' mental health and children's behavioral responses, and how those fluctuations may influence how and why media use patterns differ across and within families. Based on the DREAMER framework, it is necessary to consider the reasons why parents use media for themselves and why they provide it to their children. Specifically, research on motivations should consider how parents evaluate the risks and resources that they have surrounding media use. Research also needs to consider parent and child responses to media – including parental fluctuations in daily stress, or child difficulty transitioning from media. These dynamic patterns of use have not been empirically examined.

Other factors such as parent burnout may also influence instrumental media use decisions and may fluctuate throughout the day influencing child media use. Parent burnout is defined by three key factors surrounding parenting: exhaustion, being overwhelmed, and emotional distancing from one's children (Kerr et al., 2021a) because of a chronic imbalance of risks and resources available to parents (Kerr et al., 2021b; Roskam et al., 2021). As such, parent burnout has significant consequences for the family system and has been associated with higher parental stress, parents' suicidal and escape ideations, and fewer positive child interactions (Kerr et al., 2021b; Mikolajczak et al., 2023). The DREAMER framework could be applied to conceptualize media use as both a potential resource (e.g., to take a break or seek parenting support) and a potential risk (e.g., a source of cognitive load or venue for negative social comparison). Future research should examine daily burnout as a proximal factor with regard to parent decision-making around their own and their children's media use.

Here we provided just a few examples to illustrate how the DREAMER framework could be used to understand the ways in which parent characteristics can influence the amount, quality, and effects of children's media use. Most research ignores the interdependence of family members' media use, characterizing media use as an opportunity cost for children while ignoring causes and consequences for parents. It remains unclear whether, and under what conditions, the potential gains resulting from parent and child media use outweigh the potential costs. This critical gap in the literature precludes evidence-informed policies and interventions to support parents' healthy coping and children's development in the digital age.

6.2 Developmental Cascades

Researchers need to examine developmental cascades (Bornstein, 2009; Bornstein et al., 2013). A major problem in the field is a lack of longitudinal studies that use standardized, scalable, comprehensive measures to precisely measure the content and context of media exposure across multiple timescales. Future research should examine bidirectional links between content quality, media responses states, and socioemotional outcomes over time. Previous research has shown positive cross-sectional associations between parental use of media to regulate children's emotions and toddlers' negative affect and socioemotional difficulties (Coyne et al., 2021; Radesky et al., 2016d). Moreover, bidirectional effects of child temperament and media use have been demonstrated (McDaniel & Radesky, 2018). However, longitudinal studies are needed to understand the direction of parent regulatory media use and child outcomes as children's behavior problems and use of media to regulate may influence each other in a transactional manner (Gordon-Hacker & Gueron-Sela, 2020). For example, parents may soothe fussier children using screen media, which decreases interpersonal communication and opportunities for social exchanges that promote children's self-regulatory abilities and contributes to continued behavioral difficulties (Coyne et al., 2021; Gueron-Sela & Gordon-Hacker, 2020; Radesky et al., 2014b). Therefore, investigation of longitudinal, bidirectional interactions of child regulatory uses of media with broader measures of social competence and emotion regulation development is needed in toddlerhood, because this is a period in early childhood when children start to exhibit more behavioral negativity (Briggs Gowan et al., 2006) and there are increasing demands for preferred media (Christakis & Zimmerman, 2006). One child outcome that may exacerbate child emotion regulation is sleep. Sleep is affected by media content (Garrison et al., 2011) and has far-reaching implications for child outcomes (Seehagen et al., 2015). As such, empirical attention to the quantity and quality of child sleep is needed as part of any studies of child socioemotional well-being, including studies of media effects. Longitudinal studies that include intensive design elements that examine daily fluctuations in behaviors and media use patterns will provide information regarding the cascading consequences of changes to sleep or emotion regulation on longer-term developmental outcomes.

6.3 Pathways to Healthy and Problematic Media Use

Informed by the IT-CPU, the DREAMER framework also predicts that there will be cumulative effects of media exposure which will also have differential effects on individuals which may result in better or worse outcomes. Many individuals thrive in the digital world developing a healthy relationship with media, where media facilitate, but does not dominate, aspects of social, emotional, and physical development. However, for approximately 10% of adolescents and adults, media use has been described as pathological (Gentile, 2009).

Identifying early risk factors for later problematic media use patterns is critical in light of findings that problematic media use is associated with a range of negative outcomes later in life. Research during adolescence and emerging adulthood suggests that impulsivity, attention problems, anxiety, and poor emotion regulation all predict the development of pathological video game use (Gentile et al., 2011). Pathological use is later associated with significant negative outcomes, including decreased life satisfaction (Lemmens et al., 2009), poorer academic achievement (Gentile, 2009), increased anxiety and depression (Andreassen et al., 2016), decreased social behaviors (Limtrakul et al., 2018), and diminished sleep quality (Twenge et al., 2017).

These findings have led several major health organizations, including the American Psychiatric Association (APA) and the World Health Organization (WHO), to consider classifying pathological use of various media as a new clinical disorder (Parekh, 2018; WHO, 2018). Problematic media use may impact the development of social competence over time, and the effects may be both cumulative and bidirectional. For example, Nelson et al. (2016) found that certain types of shyness predicted engagement in "problematic media" (such as pornography, gambling, and violent video game play) during emerging adulthood. However, problematic media play then predicted more shyness over time, even when controlling for initial levels of shyness. These findings show bidirectional associations between media content and individual characteristics over time.

One major limitation is that most research only considers negative trajectories and typically only at the onset of problematic use during adolescence and adulthood. However, markers of problematic media emerge early in early childhood and might be more precise indicators of long-term outcomes than quantity of media use alone. Domoff et al. (2019) identified problematic media use in early childhood that is reminiscent of many of the pathological features seen in adolescence and emerging adulthood. In studies examining media use in 4- to 11-year-old children, Domoff et al. found between 8% and 18% of children showed evidence of problematic media use (depending on the symptom measured). Problematic media use was also related to more peer relationship problems, hyperactivity and inattention, emotional symptoms, and conduct problems (Domoff et al., 2019). This finding has been replicated in preschoolers in New Zealand and the United States (Swit et al., 2023) and was related to parenting factors with less closeness and higher parent–child conflict associated with more child problematic media use.

Although problematic media use may be associated with poor child functioning, according to both the IT-CPU and DSMM theories, some children might be more susceptible to developing and maintaining problematic media use. For example, children who are rated as fussy or intense criers or who show poor emotion-regulation are exposed to media at higher than recommended levels by their parents (Radesky et al., 2016d; Thompson et al., 2013). Similarly, children who have an emotion-regulation deficit, who might be highly impulsive and struggle to regulate their behavior, might struggle to disconnect from media or get very upset when digital media are taken away (Coyne et al., 2022b; Domoff, 2019). Thus, lower emotion-regulation might be related to increased problematic media use over time. Problematic media use in turn may exacerbate emotion dysregulation.

Future research is needed to examine the trajectory of problematic media use to determine possible preventative intervention windows. Based on the DREAMER framework, such a longitudinal approach would also need to consider other factors. Specifically, studies of problematic media use often fail to consider the potential benefits of media usage for different children. It is possible that educational content and JME may buffer negative outcomes, particularly for children who struggle with emotion regulation and may request more and be provided with more media by their parents. Potentially, use of educational content and JME could lead to a positive upward cascade for both parents and children. Thus, to understand the developmental outcomes of media and how trajectories in media use might diverge, researchers need to examine the patterns and trajectories of media use and both risks and benefits beginning during early childhood, when media habits are first formed.

6.4 More Precise and Efficient Measurement of Digital Media Use

Some researchers are exploring how to capture precise measurement of both parents' and children's media exposure, such as using wearable devices. For example, very young children can wear glasses and lapel pins for long periods of time that can hold blue light sensors (Willis et al., 2022). Media devices emit more blue light than natural daylight and could be used to calibrate when children are using devices throughout the day, analogous to how actigraphy watches detect movement patterns (Willis et al., 2022). Others have used LENA (Language ENvironment Analysis) devices, which use algorithms to track language input, language output, conversational turns, and digital speech (e.g., from a TV program or podcast). Machine learning algorithms is another promising method but has yet to be refined for broad use. For example, the LENA algorithms for media also detect white noise, such as the sound of air conditioning, and the algorithm cannot distinguish between overlapping sources of speech (e.g., talking while a TV program plays in the background), making it impossible to capture verbal interactions that occur during media use. Ultimately, researchers will be able to determine the most effective and efficient ways to detect who is using what content and with whom by triangulating these different approaches and establishing the convergence and accuracy of different approaches.

Such approaches may be able to detect whether and when digital media are used, but additional steps are needed to capture and code media content.

Capturing, operationalizing, and analyzing the content and context of media exposure are labor-intensive. For example, content analysis often requires dedicated teams to manually view content. Researchers have conducted content analyses using trained observers to detect approaches to learning in infant-directed videos (e.g., Fenstermacher et al., 2010a, 2010b) and educational and language information in preschool content (Linebarger et al., 2017). Common Sense Media has been coding the content of television programs, apps, and other media since ~2017 and has compiled an extensive, frequently updated database (www.commonsensemedia.org/) describing the quality of video content and apps. Researchers have then manually extracted these ratings to create content codes (Coyne et al., 2021). To code YouTube videos, up to 15 minutes per video is viewed to assess qualities such as commercial content, violence, or stereotypes (Radesky et al., 2020c). A similar approach is needed to code mobile apps. For example, each app can be downloaded and played for 15 minutes and then coded by trained observers using coding schemes for design abuses and Science of Learning principles (Meyer et al., 2021; Tables 1 and 2).

These manual content coding approaches are not sustainable in the long run, particularly because children may view multiple video streaming options, use hundreds of different apps, or watch thousands of different YouTube videos over the course of a longitudinal study (Radesky et al., 2020a). In addition, content is generated so quickly that content analyses are quickly obsolete. Researchers are exploring ways to increase the efficiency of content coding by developing machine learning classifiers, which may be trained to use rapidly extracted media features (e.g., free versus paid, commercialized content, category in the app store) to predict high-quality, positive, child-centered content versus low-quality content that had been manually coded. For example, researchers developed a machine learning reading comprehension algorithm to assess academic content for school-aged children in YouTube Kids videos (Kumar et al., 2023). Such approaches may also be able to determine whether content matters more in some contexts than in others (e.g., when using media to keep children occupied versus regulating children's emotions and behavior). If feasible and reliable classifiers can be built based on evidence-based quality codes, then the same indicators could be applied to newly generated content.

In addition to developing efficient and adaptive ways to code media content, researchers need to better understand how digital media are being processed by the brain using neuroimaging and physiological measures. Research has already established that infants are slower to process 2D images than 3D objects (Carver et al., 2006). EEG studies show that infants show mu rhythm, critical to social learning, while encoding live actions but not videos (Ruysschaert et al., 2013). Furthermore, hyperscanning studies have shown that brain synchrony between parents and their young children, which is associated with better learning, decreases when interactions occur via screens rather than face-to-face (Schwartz et al., 2022). Hashmi and colleagues (2020) examined activation patterns in 4- to 8-year-old children as they engaged in either play with real objects (dolls) or a tablet game either by themselves or while engaging with a peer. While they found no difference between media and non-media-based play, they found differences in activation patterns as a function of joint play versus solo play. There may be differences in neural responses while using interactive media (e.g., digital games) versus viewing traditional media (e.g., television programs), with interactive media engaging the dorsal attention network (associated with rote memorization and skill building) and traditional media engaging the default mode network (associated with concept learning and integration with prior knowledge; Anderson & Davidson, 2019), but this hypothesis has not been tested empirically. Together, studies suggest the developing brain at least sometimes processes information differently when presented in 2D versus 3D, but there may be differences based on the type of media activity, and specific brain-behavior links have not been established.

6.5 Collaborative and Synergistic Science

Other developmental fields (e.g., https://manybabies.org/) have significantly advanced via collaborative team science by developing and refining measurement tools and sharing data collectively to provide enough power to run advanced and sophisticated statistical models that consider multiple effects on child outcomes and allow for tests of replicability. Similarly, researchers studying the causes and consequences of early digital media use should take a synergistic approach, adopting similar methods and harmonizing across datasets. It will be necessary to fully embrace data sharing for data reuse and building shared data analytic tools to speed data integration and cleaning. Child development media researchers have an immediate need for collaborative platforms where complex data can be stored, cleaned, integrated, and analyzed. Collaboration between institutions in different geographic regions allows inclusion of more diverse populations that are traditionally underrepresented in media research (Katz et al., 2017; Ward et al., 2020).

As described in this Element, progress in the family media ecology has been limited by imprecise measurement and by a lack of a mechanism to rapidly share and analyze results in a theoretically driven manner. The CAFE Toolkit is an example of comprehensive measures that can better capture household media patterns in terms of parental attitudes, time use, and passive sensing. Future work could expand this effort to include some of the goals described here, such as creating automated tools for classifying digital media content and sharing those tools for use by other researchers.

7 Conclusions

Family media ecology is complex and dynamic. Each member of the family is by definition involved; parents, siblings, and extended family are connected to one another by multiple forms of media from the beginning of life such that digital media are embedded in family ecology rather than external to it. The DREAMER framework goes beyond the family media context to consider relational processes with family ecology that shape and are shaped by media use. Individual differences in parents and children as well as structural factors external to the family, like economic resources, availability of broadband networks, and unexpected perturbations to family life such as COVID-19, all contribute to the ways in which digital media are used and the impacts that digital media use has on young children in the short term and the long term. Moreover, the processes driving media use are poorly understood. It is critical to understand both the immediate, momentary factors that relate to media decisions and processes in real time and the longer-term, bidirectional associations between media use and parent and child factors within the family context. Such information is necessary to provide stakeholders, including parents, educators, and healthcare providers with clear information to navigate media usage. Furthermore, policymakers and industry need to play a much bigger role in regulation and enhancement of media services to provide a safe digital space for young children and their families. We argue that a better understanding of early media use patterns will allow us to create a digital space in which all children can thrive.

References

Abels, M., Vanden Abeele, M. M. P., Van Telgen, T., & Van Meijl, H. (2018). Nod, nod, ignore: An exploratory observational study on the relation between parental mobile media use and parental responsiveness towards young children. In E. M. Luef & M. M. Marin (eds.), *The Talking Species* (pp. 195–228). Graz: Uni-press Verlag.

Anand, S., & Krosnick, J. A. (2005). Demographic predictors of media use among infants, toddlers, and preschoolers. *American Behavioral Scientist, 48*(5), 539–561. https://doi.org/10.1177/0002764204271512.

Anderson, D. R., & Davidson, M. C. (2019). Receptive versus interactive video screens: A role for the brain's default mode network in learning from media. *Computers in Human Behavior, 99*, 168–180. https://doi.org/10.1016/j.chb.2019.05.008.

Anderson, D. R., Field, D. E., Collins, P. A., Lorch, E. P., & Nathan, J. G. (1985). Estimates of young children's time with television: A methodological comparison of parent reports and time-lapse video home observation. *Child Development, 56*, 1345–1357. https://doi.org/10.1111/j.1467-8624.1985.tb00202.x.

Anderson D. R., Hanson K. G. (2017). "Screen media and parent–child interactions" in *Media exposure during infancy and early childhood: The effects of content and context on learning and development*. eds. Barr R., Linebarger D. N. (New York: Springer;), 173–194. https://doi.org/10.1007/978-3-319-45102-2_11.

Anderson, D. R., Huston, A. C., Schmitt, K. L., Linebarger, D. L., & Wright, J. C. (2001). Early childhood television viewing and adolescent behavior: The recontact study. *Monographs of the Society for Research in Child Development, 66*(1), 1–147. https://doi.org/10.1111/1540-5834.00120.

Andreassen, C. S., Billieux, J., Griffiths, M. D. et al. (2016). The relationship between addictive use of social media and video games and symptoms of psychiatric disorders: A large-scale cross-sectional study. *Psychology of Addictive Behaviors, 30*(2), 252–262. https://doi.org/10.1037/adb0000160.

Auxier, B., Anderson, M., Perrin, A., & Turner, E. (2020). Parenting children in the age of screens. *Pew Research Center.* Washington, DC (July 18, 2020). www.pewresearch.org/internet/2020/07/28/parenting-children-in-the-age-of-screens/.

Bank, A. M., Barr, R., Calvert, S. L. et al. (2012). Maternal depression and family media use: A questionnaire and diary analysis. *Journal of Child and Family Studies, 21*, 208–216. https://doi.org/10.1007/s10826-011-9464-1.

Barr, R. (2010c). Transfer of learning between 2D and 3D sources during infancy: Informing theory and practice. *Developmental Review, 30*, 128–154. https://doi.org/10.1016/j.dr.2010.03.001.

Barr, R. (2013). Memory constraints on infant learning from picture books, television, and touchscreens. *Child Development Perspectives*, *7*, 205–210. https://doi.org/10.1111/cdep.12041.

Barr, R. (2019a). Growing up in the digital age: Early learning and family media ecology. *Current Directions in Psychological Science*, *28*, 341–346. https://doi.org/10.1177/0963721419838245.

Barr, R. (2019b). Parenting in the digital age. In M. Bornstein (ed.), *Handbook of Parenting Volume 5: The Practice of Parenting* (*3rd ed.)* (pp. 380–408). New York: Routledge.

Barr, R. (2022). Building equitable access and inclusion for children growing up in the digital age. *Policy Insights from Behavioral and Brain Sciences*, *9*(1), 73–80. https://doi.org/10.1177/23727322211068388

Barr, R., Danziger, C., Hilliard, M., Andolina, C., & Ruskis J. (2010b). Amount, content and context of infant media exposure: A parental questionnaire and diary analysis. *International Journal of Early Years Education*, *18*, 107–122. https://doi.org/10.1080/09669760.2010.494431.

Barr, R., & Hayne, H. (1999). Developmental changes in imitation from television during infancy. *Child Development*, *70*, 1067–1081. https://doi.org/10.1111/1467-8624.00079.

Barr, R., & Kirkorian, H. (2023). Reexamining models of early learning in the digital age: Applications for learning in the wild. *Journal of Applied Research in Memory and Cognition*, *12*(4), 457–472. https://doi.org/10.1037/mac0000132.

Barr, R., Kirkorian, H., Radesky, J. et al. (2020). Beyond screen time: A synergistic approach to a more comprehensive assessment of family media exposure during early childhood. *Frontiers in Psychology*, *11*, 01283. https://doi.org/10.3389/fpsyg.2020.01283.

Barr, R., Lauricella, A., Zack, E., & Calvert, S. L. (2010a). The relation between infant exposure to television and executive functioning, cognitive skills, and school readiness at age four. *Merrill Palmer Quarterly*, *56*, 21–48. www.jstor.org/stable/23098082.

Barr, R. & Linebarger, D. L. (Eds. 2017). *Media Exposure During Infancy and Early Childhood: The Effect of Content and Context on Learning and Development*. New York: Springer. https://doi.org/10.1007/978-3-319-45102-2.

Bellagamba, F., Presaghi, P., Di Marco, M. et al. (2021). How infant and toddlers' media use is related to sleeping habits in everyday life in Italy.

Frontiers in Psychology, *12*, 589664. Retrieved March 22, 2021. https://doi.org/10.3389/fpsyg.2021.589664.

Benita, N., Gordon-Hacker, A., & Gueron-Sela, N. (2020). Sleep through toddlerhood: The distinct roles of overall media use and use of media to regulate child distress. *Journal of Developmental and Behavioral Pediatrics: JDBP*, *41*(9), 690–697. https://doi.org/10.1097/DBP.0000000000000836.

Bergmann, C., Dimitrova, N., Alaslani, K. et al. (2022). Young children's screen time during the first COVID-19 lockdown in 12 countries. *Scientific Reports*, *12*(1), 2015. https://doi.org/10.1038/s41598-022-05840-5.

Bleakley, A., Jordan, A. B., & Hennessy, M. (2013). The relationship between parents' and children's television viewing. *Pediatrics*, *132*(2), e364–e371. https://doi.org/10.1542/peds.2012-3415.

Blumberg, F., & Brooks, P. (2017). *Cognitive Development in Digital Contexts*. London: Academic Press. www.elsevier.com/books/cognitive-development-in-digital-contexts/blumberg/978-0-12-809481-5.

Bornstein, M. H. (2009). Toward a model of culture↔parent↔child transactions. In A. Sameroff (ed.), *The Transactional Model of Development: How Children and Contexts Shape Each Other* (pp. 139–161). Washington, DC: American Psychological Association. https://doi.org/10.1037/11877-008.

Bornstein, M. H. (2021). *Psychological Insights for Understanding COVID-19 and Families, Parents, and Children*. New York: Routledge.

Bornstein, M. H., Hahn, C.-S., & Suwalsky, J. T. D. (2013). Language and internalizing and externalizing behavioral adjustment: Developmental pathways from childhood to adolescence. *Development and Psychopathology*, *25* (3), 857–878. https://doi.org/10.1017/S0954579413000217.

Briggs-Gowan, M. J., Carter, A. S., Bosson-Heenan, J., Guyer, A. E., Horwitz, S. M. (2006). Are infant-toddler social-emotional and behavioral problems transient? *Journal of the American Academy of Child and Adolescent Psychiatry*, *45*(7), 849–858. https://doi.org/10.1097/01.chi.0000220849.48650.59.

Bronfenbrenner, U., & Morris, P. A. (2006). The bioecological model of human development. In R. M. Lerner & W. Damon (eds.), *Handbook of Child Psychology: Theoretical Models of Human Development* (pp. 793–828). Hoboken, NJ: John Wiley & Sons.

Broderick, C. B. (1993). *Understanding Family Process: Basics of Family Systems Theory*. Thousand Oaks, CA: Sage.

Bus, A. G., Neuman, S. B., & Roskos, K. (2020). Screens, apps, and digital books for young children: The promise of multimedia. *AERA Open*, *6*(1). http://doi.org/10.1177/2332858420901494.

Calvert, S., Rideout, V., Woolard, J., Barr, R., & Strouse, G. (2005). Age, ethnicity, and socioeconomic patterns in early computer use: A national survey. *American Behavioral Scientist*, *48*, 590–607. https://doi.org/10.1177/0002764204271508.

Carroll, N., Sadowski, A., Laila, A. et al. (2020). The impact of COVID-19 on health behavior, stress, financial and food security among middle to high income Canadian families with young children. *Nutrients*, *12*(8), 2352. https://doi.org/10.3390/nu12082352.

Carver, L. J., Meltzoff, A. N., & Dawson, G. (2006). Event-related potential (ERP) indices of infants' recognition of familiar and unfamiliar objects in two and three dimensions. *Developmental Science*, *9*(1), 51–62. https://doi.org/10.1111/j.1467-7687.2005.00463.x.

Çelen Yoldas, T., & Özmert, E. N. (2021). Communicative environmental factors including maternal depression and media usage patterns on early language development. *Maternal and Child Health Journal*, *25*(6), 900–908. https://doi.org/10.1007/s10995-021-03125-3. Epub April 27, 2021.

Cheung, C. H., Bedford, R., Saez De Urabain, I. R., Karmiloff-Smith, A., & Smith, T. J. (2017). Daily touchscreen use in infants and toddlers is associated with reduced sleep and delayed sleep onset. *Scientific Reports*, *7*, 46104. https://doi.org/10.1038/srep46104.

Chindamo, S., Buja, A., DeBattisti, E. et al. (2019). Sleep and new media usage in toddlers. *European Journal of Pediatrics*, *178*, 483–490. https://doi.org/10.1007/s00431-019-03318-7.

Chonchaiya, W., Sirachairat, C., Vijakkhana, N., Wilaisakditipakorn, T., & Pruksananonda, C. (2015). Elevated background TV exposure over time increases behavioural scores of 18-month-old toddlers. *Acta Paediatrica* (*Oslo, Norway*: *1992*), *104*(10), 1039–1046. https://doi.org/10.1111/apa.13067.

Christakis, D. A., Gilkerson, J., Richards, J. A. et al. (2009). Audible television and decreased adult words, infant vocalizations, and conversational turns: A population-based study. *Archives of Pediatric and Adolescent Medicine*, *163*, 554–558. https://doi.org/10.1001/archpediatrics.2009.61.

Christakis, D. A., Ramirez, J. S. B., Ferguson, S. M., Ravinder, S., & Ramirez, J. M. (2018). How early media exposure may affect cognitive function: A review of results from observations in humans and experiments in mice. *Proceedings of the National Academy of Sciences of the United States of America*, *115*(40), 9851–9858. https://doi.org/10.1073/pnas.1711548115.

Christakis, D. A., & Zimmerman, F. J. (2006). Early television viewing is associated with protesting turning off the television at age 6. *Medscape General Medicine*, *8*(2), 63.

Cliff, D. P., Howard, S. J., Radesky, J. S., McNeill, J., & Vella, S. A. (2018). Early childhood media exposure and self-regulation: Bidirectional longitudinal associations. *Academic Pediatrics*, *18*(7), 813–819. https://doi.org/10.1016/j.acap.2018.04.012.

Connell, S. L., Lauricella, A. R., & Wartella, E. (2015). Parental co-use of media technology with their parents in the U.S.A. *Journal of Children and Media*, *9*, 5–21. https://doi.org/10.1080/17482798.2015.997440.

Conners, N., Tripathi, S., Clubb, R., & Bradley, R. (2007). Maternal characteristics associated with television viewing habits of low-income preschool children. *Journal of Child and Family Studies*, *16*(3), 415–425. https://doi.org/10.1007/s10826-006-9095-0.

Coolidge, F. L., Thede, L. L., & Young, S. E. (2000). Heritability and the comorbidity of attention deficit hyperactivity disorder with behavioral disorders and executive function deficits: A preliminary investigation. *Developmental Neuropsychology*, *17*(3), 273–287. https://doi.org/10.1207/S15326942DN1703_1.

Coyne, S. M., Holmgren, H. G., Shawcroft, J. et al. (2022c). ABCs or Attack-Boom-Crash? A longitudinal analysis of associations between media content and the development of problematic media use in early childhood. *Technology, Mind, and Behavior*, *3*(4: Winter). https://doi.org/10.1037/tmb0000093.

Coyne, S., Gale, M., Ashby, S., Memmott-Elison, M. K., Holmgren, H. G., Barr, R., Christensen-Duerden, C., & Brown, S. (2023a). Media in the moment: An observational assessment of the digital media context in early childhood. *Translational Issues in Psychological Science*, *9*(3), 186–198. https://doi.org/10.1037/tps0000377

Coyne, S. M., Reschke, P. J., Stockdale, L. et al. (2023b). Silencing screaming with screens: The longitudinal relationship between media emotion regulation processes and children's emotional reactivity, emotional knowledge, and empathy. *Emotion*, *23*(8), 2194–2204. https://doi.org/10.1037/emo0001222.

Coyne, S. M., Rogers, A., Holmgren, H. G. et al. (2023c). Masters of media: A longitudinal study of parental media efficacy, media monitoring, and child problematic media use across early childhood. *Journal of Children and Media*, *17*(3), 318–335. https://doi.org/10.1080/17482798.2023.2200958.

Coyne, S. M., Rogers, A., Shawcroft, J. et al. (2022b). Meltdowns and Media: Moment-to-moment fluctuations in young children's media use transitions and the role of children's mood state. *Computers in Human Behavior. 136*, 107360, https://doi.org/10.1016/j.chb.2022.107360.

Coyne, S. M., Shawcroft, J., Gale, M. et al. (2021). Tantrums, toddlers and technology: temperament, media emotion regulation, and problematic media use in early childhood. *Computers in Human Behavior, 120*, 106762. https://doi.org/10.1016/j.chb.2021.106762.

Coyne, S. M., Shawcroft, J., Gale, M. et al. (2022a). Digital distraction or accessible aid? Parental media use during feedings and parent-infant attachment, dysfunction, and relationship quality. *Computers in Human Behavior, 127*, 107051. https://doi.org/10.1016/j.chb.2021.107051.

Deater-Deckard, K., Wang, Z., Chen, N., & Bell, M. A. (2012). Maternal executive function, harsh parenting, and child conduct problems. *Journal of Child Psychology and Psychiatry, 53*(10), 1084–1091. https://doi.org/10.1111/j.1469-7610.2012.02582.x.

Deater-Deckard K. (2014). Family matters: Intergenerational and interpersonal processes of executive function and attentive behavior. *Current Directions in Psychological Science, 23*(3) 230–236. https://doi.org/10.1177/0963721414531597.

Domoff, S. E., Borgen, A. L., & Radesky, J. S. (2020). Interactional theory of childhood problematic media use. *Human Behavior and Emerging Technologies, 2*(4), 343–353. https://doi.org/10.1002/hbe2.217.

Domoff, S. E., Harrison, K., Gearhardt, A. N. et al. (2019). Development and validation of the Problematic Media Use Measure: A parent report measure of screen media "addiction" in children. *Psychology of Popular Media Culture, 8*, 2–11. https://doi.org/10.1037/ppm0000163.

Dore, R. A., Hassinger-Das, B., Brezack, N. et al. (2018). The parent advantage in fostering children's e-book comprehension. *Early Childhood Research Quarterly, 44*, 24–33. https://doi.org/10.1016/j.ecresq.2018.02.002.

Dore, R. A., Logan, J., Lin, T. J., Purtell, K. M., & Justice, L. (2020). Characteristics of children's media use and gains in language and literacy skills. *Frontiers in Psychology, 11*, 2224. https://doi.org/10.3389/fpsyg.2020.02224.

Eales, L., Gillespie, S., Alstat, R. A., Ferguson, G. M., & Carlson, S. M. (2021). Children's screen and problematic media use in the United States before and during the COVID-19 pandemic. *Child Development, 92*(5), O866–O882. https://doi.org/10.1111/cdev.13652.

Elias, N., Lemish, D., Dalyot, S., & Floegel, D. (2021). "Where are you?" An observational exploration of parental technoference in public places in the US and Israel. *Journal of Children and Media, 15*(3), 376–388. https://doi.org/10.1080/17482798.2020.1815228.

Ewin, C. A., Reupert, A., McLean, L. A., & Ewin, C. J. (2021). Mobile devices compared to non-digital toy play: The impact of activity type on the quality and quantity of parent language. *Computers in Human Behavior, 118*, 106669. https://doi.org/10.1016/j.chb.2020.106669.

Eyal, N. (2014). *Hooked: How to Build Habit-Forming Products*. London: Penguin.

Fisch, S. M. (2000). A Capacity Model of Children's Comprehension of Educational Content on Television. *Media Psychology*, *2*(1), 63–91. https://doi.org/10.1207/S1532785XMEP0201_4

Fisch, S. M. (2017). Bridging Theory and Practice: Applying Cognitive and Educational Theory to the Design of Educational Media. In *Cognitive Development in Digital Contexts* (pp. 217–234). Elsevier. https://doi.org/10.1016/B978-0-12-809481-5.00011-0

Fenson, L., Pethick, S., Renda, C. et al. (2000). Short-form versions of the MacArthur Communicative Development Inventories. *Applied Psycholinguistics*, *21*, 95–116.

Fenstermacher, S. K., Barr, R., Brey, E. et al. (2010a). Interactional quality depicted in infant-directed videos: Where are the interactions? *Infant and Child Development*, *19*, 594–612. https://doi.org/10.1002/icd.714.

Fenstermacher, S. K., Linebarger, D., Pempek, T. A. et al. (2010b). Infant-directed media: An analysis of product information and claims. *Infant and Child Development*, *19*, 557–576. https://doi.org/10.1002/icd.718.

Fidler, A., Zack, E., & Barr, R. (2010). Television viewing patterns in 6- to 18-month-olds: The role of caregiver-infant interactional quality. *Infancy*, *15*, 176–196. https://doi.org/10.1111/j.1532-7078.2009.00013.x.

Fisch, S. M. (2000). A capacity model of children's comprehension of educational content on television. *Media Psychology*, *2*(1), 63–91. https://doi.org/10.1207/S1532785XMEP0201_4.

Fisch, S. M. (2017). Bridging theory and practice: Applying cognitive and educational theory to the design of educational media. In F. C. Blumberg, P. J. Brooks (eds.), *Cognitive Development in Digital Contexts* (pp. 217–234). London: Elsevier. https://doi.org/10.1016/B978-0-12-809481-5.00011-0.

Fogg, B. J. (2009, April). A behavior model for persuasive design. In *Proceedings of the 4th International Conference on Persuasive Technology* (pp. 1–7). Claremont, CA.

Furenes, M. I., Kucirkova, N., & Bus, A. C. (2021). A comparison of children's reading on paper versus screen: A meta-analysis. *Review of Educational Research*, *91*, 483–517. https://doi.org/10.3102/0034654321998074.

Galvin, K. M., Dickson, F. C., & Marrow, S. R. (2006). Systems theory: Patterns and (w)holes in family communication. In D. O. Braithwaite & L. A. Baxter (eds.), *Engaging Theories in Family Connection: Multiple Perspectives* (pp. 309–324). Thousand Oaks, CA: Sage.

Gardner, M. F. (1990). *EOWPVT-R: Expressive One-word Picture Vocabulary Test, Revised*. Novato, CA: Academic Therapy.

Garrison, M. M., Liekweg, K., & Christakis, D. A. (2011). Media use and child sleep: The impact of content, timing, and environment. *Pediatrics*, *128*, 29–35. http://doi.org/10.1542/peds.2010-3304.

Gaudreau, C., Hirsh-Pasek, K., & Golinkoff, R. M. (2022). What's in a distraction? The effect of parental cell phone use on parents' and children's question-asking. *Developmental Psychology*, *58*(1), 55–68. https://doi.org/10.1037/dev0001268.

Gentile, D. A. (2009). Pathological video game use among youth 8 to 18: A national study. *Psychological Science*, *20*(6), 594–602. https://doi.org/10.1111/j.1467-9280.2009.02382.x.

Gentile, D. A., Choo, H., Liau, A. et al. (2011). Pathological video game use among youths: A two-year longitudinal study. *Pediatrics*, *127*(2), e319–e329. https://doi.org/10.1542/peds.2010-1353.

Goh, S. N., Teh, L. H., Tay, W. R. et al. (2016). Sociodemographic, home environment and parental influences on total and device-specific screen viewing in children aged 2 years and below: An observational study. *British Medical Journal Open*, *6*, e009113. http://doi/org/10.1136/bmjopen-2015-009113.

Goldstein, M. H., Schwade, J. A., & Bornstein, M. H. (2009). The value of vocalizing: Five-month-old infants associate their own noncry vocalizations with responses from caregivers. *Child Development*, *80*(3), 636–644. https://doi.org/10.1111/j.1467-8624.2009.01287.x.

Gordon-Hacker, A., & Gueron-Sela, N. (2020). Maternal use of media to regulate child distress: A double-edged sword? Longitudinal links to toddlers' negative emotionality. *Cyberpsychology, Behavior and Social Networking*, *23*(6), 400–405. https://doi.org/10.1089/cyber.2019.0487.

Gray, C. M., Kou, Y., Battles, B., Hoggatt, J., & Toombs A. L. (2018). The dark (patterns) side of UX design. CHI '18: Proceedings of the 2018 CHI Conference on Human Factors in Computing Systems. April 2018, Paper No.: 534, 1–14.

Gueron-Sela, N., & Gordon-Hacker, A. (2020). Longitudinal links between media use and focused attention through toddlerhood: A cumulative risk approach. *Frontiers in Psychology*, *11*, 569222. https://doi.org/10.3389/fpsyg.2020.569222.

Gueron-Sela, N., Shalev, I., Gordon-Hacker, A., Egutobov, A., & Barr, R. (2023). Screen media exposure and behavioral adjustment in early childhood during and after COVID-19 home lockdown periods. *Computers in Human Behavior*, *140*, 107572 https://doi.org/10.1016/j.chb.2022.107572.

Hashmi, S., Vanderwert, R. E., Price, H. A., & Gerson, S. A. (2020). Exploring the benefits of doll play through neuroscience. *Frontiers in Human Neuroscience*, *14*, 560176. https://doi.org/10.3389/fnhum.2020.560176

Hartshorne, J. K., Huang, Y. T., Lucio Paredes, P. M. et al. (2021). Screen time as an index of family distress. *Current Research in Behavioral Sciences*, *2*, 100023. https://doi.org/10.1016/j.crbeha.2021.100023.

Hedderson, M. M., Bekelman, T. A., Li, M. et al. (2023). Trends in screen time use among children during the COVID-19 pandemic, July 2019 through August 2021. *JAMA Network Open*, *6*(2), e2256157. https://doi.org/10.1001/jamanetworkopen.2022.56157.

Heimann, M., Hedendahl, L., Ottmer, E. et al. (2021). 2-year-olds learning from 2D media with and without parental support: Comparing two forms of joint media engagement with passive viewing and learning from 3D. *Frontiers in Psychology*, *11*, 576940. https://doi.org/10.3389/fpsyg.2020.576940.

Hiniker, A., Heung, S. S., Hong, S., & Kientz, J. A. (2018a, April). Coco's videos: An empirical investigation of video-player design features and children's media use. In *Proceedings of the 2018 CHI Conference on Human Factors in Computing Systems* (pp. 1–13). Montreal.

Hiniker, A., Lee, B., Kientz, J. A., & Radesky, J. S. (2018b, April). Let's play! Digital and analog play between preschoolers and parents. In *Proceedings of the 2018 CHI Conference on Human Factors in Computing Systems* (pp. 1–13). Montreal. https://doi.org/10.1145/3173574.3174233.

Hiniker, A., Sobel, K., Suh, H. et al. (2015). Texting while parenting: How adults use mobile phones while caring for children at the playground. *Proceedings of the 33rd Annual ACM Conference on Human Factors in Computing Systems*, 727–736. https://doi.org/10.1145/2702123.2702199.

Hinkley, T., Verbestel, V., Ahrens, W. et al. (2014). Early childhood electronic media use as a predictor of poorer well-being: A prospective cohort study. *JAMA Pediatrics*, *168*(5), 485–492. https://doi.org/10.1001/jamapediatrics.2014.94.

Hipp, D., Gerhardstein, P., Zimmermann, L. et al. (2017). The dimensional divide: Learning from TV and touchscreens during early childhood. In R. Barr and D. Linebarger (eds.), *Media Exposure during Infancy and Early Childhood* (pp. 33–54). Cham: Springer. https://doi.org/10.1007/978-3-319-45102-2_3.

Hirsh-Pasek, K., Zosh, J. M., Golinkoff, R. M. et al. (2015). Putting education in "educational" apps: Lessons from the science of learning. *Psychological Science in the Public Interest : A Journal of the American Psychological Society*, *16*, 3–34. https://doi.org/10.1177/1529100615569721.

Holmgren, H. G., Stockdale, L., Gale, M., & Coyne, S. M. (2022). Parent and child problematic media use: The role of maternal postpartum depression and dysfunctional parent-child interactions in young children. *Computers in Human Behavior*, *133*, 107293. https://doi.org/10.1016/j.chb.2022.107293.

Jing, M., Ye, T., Kirkorian, H. L., & Mares, M.-L. (2023). Screen media exposure and young children's vocabulary learning and development: A meta-analysis. *Child Development*, *94*, 1398–1418. https://doi.org/10.1111/cdev.13927.

Kabali, H. K., Irigoyen, M. M., Nunez-Davis, R. et al. (2015). Exposure and use of mobile media devices by young children. *Pediatrics*, *136*(6), 1044–1050. https://doi.org/10.1542/peds.2015-2151.

Karasik, L., Tamis-LeMonda, C. S., & Adolph, K. (2016). Decisions at the brink: Locomotor experience affects infants' use of social information on an adjustable drop-off. *Frontiers in Psychology*, *7*, 797. https://doi.org/10.3389/fpsyg.2016.00797.

Katz, V., Gonzalez, C., & Clark, K. (2017). Digital inequality and developmental trajectories of low income, immigrant, and minority children. *Pediatrics*, *140*(Supplement 2), 132–136. S132–S136. https://doi.org/10.1542/peds.2016-1758R.

Katz, V. S., Jordan, A. B., & Ognyanova, K. (2021). Digital inequality, faculty communication, and remote learning experiences during the COVID-19 pandemic: A survey of U.S. undergraduates. *PLOS ONE*, *16*(2), e0246641. https://doi.org/10.1371/journal.pone.0246641.

Katz, V. S., Moran, M. B., & Ognyanova, K. (2019). Contextualizing connectivity: How internet connection type and parental factors influence technology use among lower-income children. *Information, Communication & Society*, *22*(3), 313–335. https://doi.org/10.1080/1369118X.2017.1379551.

Kerr, M. L., Rasmussen, H. F., Borelli, J. L., Buttitta, K. V., & Smiley, P. A. (2021a). Exploring the complexity of mothers' real-time emotions while caregiving. *Emotion*, *21*(3), 545–556. http://dx.doi.org/10.1037/emo0000719.

Kerr, M. L., Rasmussen, H. F., Smiley, P. A. et al. (2021b). Within- and between-family differences in mothers' guilt and shame: Caregiving, coparenting, and attachment. *Journal of Family Psychology*, *35*(3), 265–275. http://dx.doi.org/10.1037/fam0000647.

Kiefner-Burmeister, A., Domoff, S., & Radesky, J. (2020). Feeding in the digital age: An observational analysis of mobile device use during family meals at fast food restaurants in Italy. *International Journal of Environmental Research and Public Health*, *17*(17), 6077. https://doi.org/10.3390/ijerph17176077.

Kirkorian, H., & Barr, R. (2021). CAFE consortium toolkit documentation. *Databrary*. http://doi.org/10.17910/b7.1372.

Kirkorian, H. L. (2018). When and how do interactive digital media help children connect what they see on and off the screen? *Child Development Perspectives*, *12*, 210–214. https://doi.org/10.1111/cdep.12290.

Kirkorian, H. L., Choi, K., & Anderson, D. R. (2019). American parents' active involvement mediates the impact of background television on young children's toy play. *Journal of Children and Media, 19*, 377–394. https://doi.org/10.1080/17482798.2019.1635033.

Kirkorian, H. L., Pempek, T. A., Murphy, L. A., Schmidt, M. E., & Anderson, D. R. (2009). The impact of background television on parent-child interaction. *Child Development, 80*, 1350–1359. https://doi.org/10.1111/j.1467-8624.2009.01337.x.

Konrad, C., Berger-Hanke, M., Hassel, G., & Barr, R. (2021a). Does texting interrupt learning in 19-month-old infants? *Infant Behavior and Development, 62*, 101513 https://doi.org/10.1016/j.infbeh.2020.101513.

Konrad, C., Hillmann, M., Rispler, J. et al. (2021b). Quality of mother-child interaction before, during and after smartphone use. *Frontiers*. https://doi.org/10.3389/fpsyg.2021.616656.

Kostyrka-Allchorne, K., Cooper, N. R., & Simpson, A. (2017). The relationship between television exposure and children's cognition and behaviour: A systematic review. *Developmental Review, 44*, 19–58. https://doi.org/10.1016/j.dr.2016.12.002.

Krapf-Bar, D., Davidovitch, M., Rozenblatt-Perkal, Y., & Gueron-Sela, N. (2022). Maternal mobile phone use during mother-child interactions interferes with the process of establishing joint attention. *Developmental Psychology, 58*(9), 1639–1651. https://doi.org/10.1037/dev0001388.

Krcmar, M., & Cingel, D. P. (2014). Parent–child joint reading in traditional and electronic formats. *Media Psychology, 17*(3), 262–281. https://doi.org/10.1080/15213269.2013.840243.

Kucirkova, N., Littleton, K., & Kyparissiadis, A. (2018). The influence of children's gender and age on children's use of digital media at home. *British Journal of Educational Technology, 49*, 545–559. https://doi.org/10.1111/bjet.12543.

Kumar, S., Mallikarjuna T., & Khudabukhsh, A. (2023). Quantifying the academic quality of children's videos using machine comprehension, 2023. *IEEE Transactions on Knowledge and Data Engineering*. https://doi.org/10.48550/arXiv.2303.17201.

Lauricella, A., Barr, R., & Calvert, S. (2009). Computer skills: Influences of young children's executive functioning abilities and parental scaffolding techniques in the US. *Journal of Children and Media, 3*, 217–233. https://doi.org/10.1080/1748279090299989.

Lauricella, A. R., Blackwell, C. K., & Wartella, E. (2017). The "new" technology environment: The role of content and context on learning and development from mobile media. In R. Barr & D. Linebarger (eds.), *Media Exposure during Infancy and Early Childhood: The Effect of Content and Context on Learning and Development* (pp. 1–24). New York: Springer. https://doi.org/10.1007/978-3-319-45102-2_1.

Lauricella, A., Calvert, S., & Barr, R. (2014). Parent-child interactions during traditional and computer book reading for children's story comprehension. *International Journal of Child-Computer Interaction*, *2*, 17–25. https://doi.org/10.1016/j.ijcci.2014.07.001.

Lauricella, A. R., Cingel, D. P., Beaudoin-Ryan, L. et al . (2016). *The Common Sense Census: Plugged-In Parents of Tweens and Teens*. San Francisco, CA: Common Sense Media.

Lauricella, A. R., Wartella, E., & Rideout, V. J. (2015). Young children's screen time: The complex role of parent and child factors. *Journal of Applied Developmental Psychology*, *36*, 11–17. https://doi.org/10.1016/j.appdev.2014.12.001.

Lavigne, H. J., Hanson, K. G., & Anderson, D. R. (2015). The influence of television coviewing on parent language directed at toddlers. *Journal of Applied Developmental Psychology*, *36*, 1–10. https://doi.org/10.1016/j.appdev.2014.11.004.

Lemmens, J. S., Valkenburg, P. M., & Peter, J. (2009). Development and validation of a game addiction scale for adolescents. *Media Psychology*, *12* (1), 77–95. https://doi.org/10.1080/15213260802669458.

Limtrakul, N., Louthrenoo, O., Narkpongphun, A., Boonchooduang, N., & Chonochaiya, W. (2018). Media use and pyschosocial adjustment in children and adolescents. *Journal of Paediatrics and Child Health*, *54*(3), 296–301. https://doi.org/10.1111/jc.13725.

Lin, L.-Y., Cherng, R.-J., Chen, Y.-J., Chen, Y.-J., & Yang, H.-M. (2015). Effects of television exposure on developmental skills among young children. *Infant Behavior and Development*, *38*, 20–26. https://doi.org/10.1016/j.infbeh.2014.12.005.

Linder, L., McDaniel, B. T., & Jaffe, H. (2022). Moment-to-moment observation of parental media use and parent-child interaction: Quality and media multitasking. *Human Behavior and Emerging Technologies*, *2022*, 1–9. https://doi.org/10.1155/2022/4896637.

Linebarger, D. L., Barr, R., Lapierre, M. A., & Piotrowski, J. T. (2014). Associations between parenting, media use, cumulative risk, and children's executive functioning. *Journal of Developmental and Behavioral Pediatrics*, *35*(6), 367–377. https://doi.org/10.1097/DBP.0000000000000069.

Linebarger, D. N., Brey, E., Fenstermacher, S. & Barr, R. (2017). What makes preschool educational television educational? A content analysis of literacy, language-promoting, and prosocial preschool programming. In R. Barr, R. &

D. N. Linebarger (Eds.). *Media Exposure During Infancy and Early Childhood: The Effect of Content and Context on Learning and Development*, pp 97–134. New York: Springer. https://doi.org/10.1007/978-3-319-45102-2_7.

Linebarger, D. L., & Vaala, S. E. (2010). Screen media and language development in infants and toddlers: An ecological perspective. *Developmental Review, 30*(2), 176–202. https://doi.org/10.1016/j.dr.2010.03.006.

Linebarger, D. L., & Walker, D. (2005). Infants' and toddlers' television viewing and language outcomes. *American Behavioral Scientist, 48*(5), 624–645.

Lund, L., Sølvhøj, I. N., Danielsen, D., & Andersen, S. (2021). Electronic media use and sleep in children and adolescents in western countries: A systematic review. *BMC Public Health, 21*(1), 1598. https://doi.org/10.1186/s12889-021-11640-9.

Madigan, S., McArthur, B. A., Anhorn, C., Eirich, R., Christakis, D. A. (2020). Associations between screen use and child language skills: A systematic review and meta-analysis. *JAMA Pediatrics, 174*(7), 665–675. https://doi.org/10.1001/jamapediatrics.2020.0327.

Makin, S. (2018). Searching for digital technology's effects on well-being. *Nature, 563*(7733), S138–S140. https://doi.org/10.1038/d41586-018-07503-w.

Mallawaarachchi, S. R., Anglim, J., Hooley, M., & Horwood, S. (2022). Associations of smartphone and tablet use in early childhood with psychosocial, cognitive and sleep factors: a systematic review and meta-analysis. *Early Childhood Research Quarterly, 60*, 13–33. https://doi.org/10.1016/j.ecresq.2021.12.008

Malti, T., & Dys, S. P. (2018). From being nice to being kind: Development of prosocial behaviors. *Current Opinion in Psychology, 20*, 45–49. https://doi.org/10.1016/j.copsyc.2017.07.036.

Markey, E. (2018). Children and Media Research Advancement Act. https://www.congress.gov/bill/109th-congress/senate-bill/1902

Mathur, A., Acar, G., Friedman, M. J. et al. (2019). Dark patterns at scale: Findings from a crawl of 11K shopping websites. *Proceedings of the ACM on Human-Computer Interaction, 3*(CSCW), 1–32. https://doi.org/10.1145/3359183.

McDaniel, B. T. (2019). Parent distraction with phones, reasons for use, and impacts on parenting and child outcomes: A review of the emerging research. *Human Behavior and Emerging Technologies, 1*(2), 72–80. https://doi.org/10.1002/hbe2.139.

McDaniel, B. T. (2020). Technoference: Parent mobile device use and implications for children and parent-child relationships. *Zero to Three, 41*(2), 30–36.

McDaniel, B. T. (2021). The DISRUPT: A measure of parent distraction with phones and mobile devices and associations with depression, stress, and parenting quality. *Human Behavior and Emerging Technologies*, *3*(5), 922–932. https://doi.org/10.1002/hbe2.267.

McDaniel, B. T., & Coyne, S. M. (2016). Technology interference in the parenting of young children: Implications for mothers' perceptions of coparenting. *The Social Science Journal*, *53*(4), 435–443. https://doi.org/10.1016/j.soscij.2016.04.010.

McDaniel, B. Y., & Radesky, J. S. (2018a). Technoference: Parent distraction with technology and associations with child behavior problems. *Child Development*, *89*(1), 100–109. https://doi.org/10.1111/cdev.12822.

McDaniel, B. T., & Radesky, J. S. (2018b). Technoference: Longitudinal associations between parent technology use, parenting stress, and child behavior problems. *Pediatric Research*, *84*(2), 210–218. https://doi.org/10.1038/s41390-018-0052-6.

McHarg, G., Ribner, A. D., Devine, R. T., & Hughes, C. (2020). Screen time and executive function in toddlerhood: A longitudinal study. *Frontiers in Psychology*, *11*, 570392. https://doi.org/10.3389/fpsyg.2020.570392.

Mendelsohn, A. L., Brockmeyer, C. A., Dreyer, B. P. et al. (2010). Do verbal interactions with infants during electronic media exposure mitigate adverse impacts on their language development as toddlers? *Infant and Child Development*, *19*(6), 577–593. https://doi.org/10.1002/icd.711.

Meyer, M., Adkins, V., Yuan, N. et al. (2019). Advertising in young children's apps: A content analysis. *Journal of Developmental & Behavioral Pediatrics*, *40*(1), 32–39. https://doi.org/10.1097/DBP.0000000000000622.

Meyer, M., Zosh, J. M., McLaren, C. et al. (2021). How educational are "educational" apps for young children? App store content analysis using the Four Pillars of Learning framework. *Journal of Children and Media*, *15* (4), 526–548. https://doi.org/10.1080/17482798.2021.1882516.

Meyer, T. J., Miller, M. L., Metzger, R. L., & Borkovec, T. D. (1990). Development and validation of the Penn State worry questionnaire. *Behavior Research and Therapy*, *28*(6), 487–495. https://doi.org/10.1016/0005-7967(90)90135-6.

Mikolajczak, M., Aunola, K., Sorkkila, M., & Roskam, I. (2023). 15 Years of parental burnout research: Systematic review and agenda. *Current Directions in Psychological Science*, *32*(4), 276–283. https://doi.org/10.1177/09637214221142777.

Mikolajczak, M., & Roskam, I. (2018). A theoretical and clinical framework for parental burnout: The balance between risks and resources (BR2). *Frontiers in Psychology*, *9*(886). https://doi.org/10.3389/fpsyg.2018.00886.

Moorman, J. D., Morgan, P., & Adams, T. L. (2019). The implications of screen media use for the sleep behavior of children ages 0–5: A systematic review of the literature. *Current Sleep Medicine Reports*, *5*(3), 164–172. https://doi.org/10.1007/s40675-019-00151-0.

Munzer, T., Torres, C., Domoff, S. E. et al. (2022). Child media use during COVID-19: Associations with contextual and social-emotional factors. *Journal of Developmental & Behavioral Pediatrics*, *43*(9), e573–e580. https://doi.org/10.1097/DBP.0000000000001125.

Munzer, T. G., Miller, A. L., Wang, Y., Kaciroti, N., & Radesky, J. (2021). Tablets, toddlers, and tantrums: The immediate effects of tablet device play. *Acta paediatrica* (*Oslo, Norway*: *1992*), *110*(1), 255–256. https://doi.org/10.1111/apa.15509.

Munzer, T. G., Miller, A. L., Weeks, H. M., Kaciroti, N., & Radesky, J. (2019). Parent-toddler social reciprocity during reading from electronic tablets vs print books. *JAMA pediatrics*, *173*(11), 1076–1083. https://doi.org/10.1001/jamapediatrics.2019.3480.

Myers, L. J., Crawford, E., Murphy, C., Aka-Ezoua, E., & Felix, C. (2018). Eyes in the room trump eyes on the screen: Effects of a responsive co-viewer on toddlers' responses to and learning from video chat. *Journal of Children and Media*, *12*(3), 275–294. https://doi.org/10.1080/17482798.2018.1425889.

Myruski, S., Gulyayeva, O., Birk, S. et al. (2018). Digital disruption? Maternal mobile device use is related to infant social-emotional functioning. *Developmental Science*, *21*(4), e12610. https://doi.org/10.1111/desc.12610.

Nabi, R. L., & Krcmar, M. (2016). It takes two: The effect of child characteristics on U.S. parents' motivations for allowing electronic media use. *Journal of Children and Media*, *10*(3), 285–303. https://doi.org/10.1080/17482798.2016.1162185.

Nairn, A., & Fine, C. (2008). Who's messing with my mind? The implications of dual-process models for the ethics of advertising to children. *International Journal of Advertising*, *27*(3):447–470. https://doi.org/10.2501/S0265048708080062.

Navarro, J. L., & Tudge, J. R. H. (2023). Technologizing Bronfenbrenner: Neo-ecological theory. *Current Psychology*, *42*(22), 19338–19354. https://doi.org/10.1007/s12144-022-02738-3.

Nelson, L. J., Coyne, S. M., Howard, E., & Clifford, B. N. (2016). Withdrawing to a virtual world: Associations between subtypes of withdrawal, media use, and maladjustment in emerging adults. *Developmental Psychology*, *52*(6), 933–942. https://doi.org/10.1037/dev0000128.

Neuman, S. B., Flynn, R., Wong, K., & Kaefer, T. (2020). Quick, incidental word learning in educational media: All contexts are not equal. *Educational*

Technology Research and Development, *68*(6), 2913–2937. https://doi.org/10.1007/s11423-020-09815-z.

Neville, R. D., McArthur, B. A., Eirich, R., Lakes, K. D., & Madigan, S. (2021). Bidirectional associations between screen time and children's externalizing and internalizing behaviors. *Journal of Child Psychology and Psychiatry*, *62* (12), 1475–1484. https://doi.org/10.1111/jcpp.13425.

NIH (2018). *Media exposure and early child development workshop*. Accessed online [June 5, 2019] www.nichd.nih.gov/sites/default/files/2018-06/Media_Exp_Early_Child_Dev_Work.pdf.

Nikken, P. (2019). Parents' instrumental use of media in childrearing: Relationships with confidence in parenting, and health and conduct problems in children. *Journal of Child and Family Studies*, *28*, 531–546. https://doi.org/10.1007/s10826-018-1281-3.

Nikken, P., & Schols, M. (2015). How and why parents guide the media use of young children. *Journal of Child and Family Studies*, *24*, 3423–3435. http://doi.org/10.1007/s10826-015-0144-4.

Ochoa, W., Reich, S. M., & Farkas, G. (2021). The observed quality of caregiver-child interactions with and without a mobile screen device. *Academic Pediatrics*, *21*(4), 620–628. https://doi.org/10.1016/j.acap.2020.07.012.

Ophir, E., Nass, C., & Wagner, A. D. (2009). Cognitive control in media multitaskers. *Proceedings of the National Academy of Sciences*, *106* (37),15583–15587. https://doi.org/10.1073/pnas.0903620106.

Ozturk Eyimaya, A., & Yalçin Irmak, A. (2021). Relationship between parenting practices and children's screen time during the COVID-19 pandemic in Turkey. *Journal of Pediatric Nursing*, *56*, 24–29. https://doi.org/10.1016/j.pedn.2020.10.002.

Padilla-Walker, L. M., Coyne, S. M., & Fraser, A. M. (2012). Getting a high-speed family connection: Associations between family media use and family connection. *Family Relations*, *61*(3), 426–440. https://doi.org/10.1111/j.1741-3729.2012.00710.x.

Pagani, L. S., Fitzpatrick, C., Barnett, T. A., & Dubow, E. (2010). Prospective associations between early childhood television exposure and academic, psychosocial, and physical well-being by middle childhood. *Archives of Pediatrics & Adolescent Medicine*, *164*(5), 425–431. https://doi.org/10.1001/archpediatrics.2010.50.

Parekh, R. (2018). *Internet Gaming*. Washington, DC: American Psychiatric Association. www.psychiatry.org/patients-families/internet-gaming.

Pearcey, S., Gordon, K., Chakrabarti, B. et al. (2021). Research review: The relationship between social anxiety and social cognition in children and adolescents: A systematic review and meta-analysis. *Journal of Child Psychology and Psychiatry*, *62*(7), 805–821. https://doi-org.erl.lib.byu.edu/10.1111/jcpp.13310.

Pearlin, L. I., Menaghan, E. G., Lieberman, M. A., & Mullan, J. T. (1981). The stress process. *Journal of Health and Social Behavior*, 337–356. https://doi.org/10.2307/2136676.

Pedrotti, B. G., Mallmann, M. Y., Almeida, C. R. S. et al. (2022). Infants' and toddlers' digital media use and mothers' mental health: A comparative study before and during the COVID-19 pandemic. *Infant Mental Health Journal*, *43*(1), 24–35. https://doi.org/10.1002/imhj.21952.

Pempek, T. A., Demers, L. B., Hanson, K., Kirkorian, H. L., & Anderson, D. R. (2011). The impact of infant-directed videos on parent-child interaction. *Journal of Applied Developmental Psychology*, *32*, 10–19. https://doi.org/10.1016/j.appdev.2010.10.001.

Pempek, T. A., & Kirkorian, H. L. (2020). Effects of background TV on early development. In J. van den Bulck (ed.), *The International Encyclopedia of Media Psychology* (pp. 1–9). Boston, MA: Wiley-Blackwell . https://doi.org/10.1002/9781119011071.iemp0222.

Pempek, T. A., Kirkorian, H. L., & Anderson, D. R. (2014). The effects of background television on the quality and quantity of child-directed speech by parents. *Journal of Children and Media*, *8*, 211–222. https://doi.org/10.1080/17482798.2014.920715.

Pempek, T. A., & McDaniel, B. T. (2016). Young children's tablet use and associations with maternal well-being. *Journal of Child and Family Studies*, *25*(8), 2636–2647. https://doi.org/10.1007/s10826-016-0413-x.

Piotrowski, J. (2017). The parental media mediation context of young children's media use. In R. Barr & D. Linebarger (eds.), *Media Exposure during Infancy and Early Childhood: The Effect of Content and Context on Learning and Development* (pp. 205–220). New York: Springer. https://doi.org/10.1007/978-3-319-45102-2_13.

Pombo, A., Luz, C., Rodrigues, L. P., & Cordovil, R. (2021). Effects of COVID-19 confinement on the household routines of children in Portugal. *Journal of Child and Family Studies*, *30*(7), 1664–1674. https://doi.org/10.1007/s10826-021-01961-z.

Przybylski, A. K., & Weinstein, N. (2019). Digital screen time limits and young children's psychological well-being: Evidence from a population-based study. *Child Development*, *90*(1), e56–e65. https://doi.org/10.1111/cdev.13007.

Radesky, J., Christakis, D., Hill, D. et al. (2016a). Media and young minds. *Pediatrics*, *138*(5), e20162591. https://doi.org/10.1542/peds.2016-2591.

Radesky, J., & Hiniker, A. (2022). From moral panic to systemic change: Making child-centered design the default. *International Journal of Child-Computer Interaction*, *31*, 100351. https://doi.org/10.1016/j.ijcci.2021.100351.

Radesky, J., Hiniker, A., McLaren, C. et al. (2022). Prevalence and characteristics of manipulative design in mobile applications used by children. *JAMA Network Open*, *5*(6), e2217641. https://doi.org/10.1001/jamanetworkopen.2022.17641.

Radesky, J., Leung, C., Appugliese, D. et al. (2018). Maternal mental representations of the child and mobile phone use during parent-child mealtimes. *Journal of Developmental & Behavioral Pediatrics*, *39*(4), 310–317. https://doi.org/10.1097/DBP.0000000000000556.

Radesky, J., Miller, A. L., Rosenblum, K. L. et al. (2015). Maternal mobile device use during a structured parent-child interaction task. *Academic Pediatrics*, *15*(2), 238–244. https://doi.org/10.1016/j.acap.2014.10.001.

Radesky, J., Reid Chassiakos, Y. R., Ameenuddin, N., Navsaria, D., & C.O.P.E. (2020b). Digital advertising to children. *Pediatrics*, *146*(1), e20201681. https://doi.org/10.1542/peds.2020-1681.

Radesky, J. S., Eisenberg, S., Kistin, C. J. et al. (2016b). Overstimulated consumers or next-generation learners? Parent tensions about child mobile technology use. *Annals of Family Medicine*, *14*(6), 503–508. https://doi.org/10.1370/afm.1976.

Radesky, J. S., Kistin, C., Eisenberg, S. et al. (2016c). Parent perspectives on their mobile technology use: The excitement and exhaustion of parenting while connected. *Journal of Developmental & Behavioral Pediatrics*, *37*(9), 694–701. https://doi.org/10.1097/DBP.0000000000000357.

Radesky, J. S., Kistin, C. J., Zuckerman, B. et al. (2014a). Patterns of mobile device use by caregivers and children during meals in fast food restaurants. *Pediatrics*, *133*(4), e843–e849. https://doi.org/10.1542/peds.2013-3703.

Radesky, J. S., Peacock-Chambers, E., Zuckerman, B., & Silverstein, M. (2016d). Use of mobile technology to calm upset children: Associations with social-emotional development. *JAMA Pediatrics*, *170*(4), 397–399. https://doi.org/10.1001/jamapediatrics.2015.4260.

Radesky, J. S., Schaller, A., Yeo, S. L., Weeks, H. M., & Robb, M. B. (2020c). Young kids and YouTube: How ads, toys, and games dominate viewing, 2020. San Francisco, CA: Common Sense Media. Published online November 17, 2020.

Radesky, J. S., Silverstein, M., Zuckerman, B., & Christakis, D. A. (2014b). Infant self-regulation and early childhood media exposure. *Pediatrics*, *133*(5), e1172–e1178. https://doi.org/10.1542/peds.2013-2367.

Radesky, J. S., Weeks, H. M., Ball, R. et al. (2020a). Young children's use of smartphones and tablets. *Pediatrics*, *146*(1), e20193518. https://doi.org/10.1542/peds.2019-3518.

Raman, S., Guerrero-Duby, S., McCullough, J. L. et al. (2017). Screen exposure during daily routines and a young child's risk for having social-emotional delay. *Clinical Pediatrics*, *56*(13), 1244–1253. https://doi.org/10.1177/0009922816684600.

Ramírez-Coronel, A. A., Abdu, W. J., Alshahrani, S. H. et al. (2023). Childhood obesity risk increases with increased screen time: A systematic review and dose-response meta-analysis. *Journal of Health, Population, and Nutrition*, *42*(1), 5. https://doi.org/10.1186/s41043-022-00344-4.

Ramsetty, A., & Adams, C. (2020). Impact of the digital divide in the age of COVID-19. *Journal of the American Medical Informatics Association: JAMIA*, *27*(7), 1147–1148. https://doi.org/10.1093/jamia/ocaa078.

Rasmussen, E. E., Shafer, A., Colwell, M. J. et al. (2016). Relation between active mediation, exposure to *Daniel Tiger's Neighborhood*, and US preschoolers' social and emotional development. *Journal of Children and Media*, *10*(4), 443–461. https://doi.org/10.1080/17482798.2016.1203806.

Reed, J., Hirsh-Pasek, K., & Golinkoff, R. M. (2017). Learning on hold: Cell phones sidetrack parent-child interactions. *Developmental Psychology*, *53* (8), 1428–1436. https://doi.org/10.1037/dev0000292.

Reid Chassiakos, Y., Radesky, J., Christakis, D. et al. (2016). Children and Adolescents and Digital Media. *Pediatrics*, *138*, e20162593. https://doi.org/10.1542/peds.2016-2593.

Ribner, A. D., Barr, R. F., & Nichols, D. L. (2020). Background media use is negatively related to language and literacy skills: Indirect effects of self-regulation. *Pediatric Research*, *89*(6), 1523–1529. https://doi.org/10.1038/s41390-020-1004-5.

Ribner, A. D., Coulanges, L., Friedman, S., Libertus, M. E., & I-FAM-Covid Consortium. (2021). Screen time in the Coronavirus 2019 era: International trends of increasing use among 3- to 7-year-old children. *The Journal of Pediatrics*, *239*, 59–66. https://doi.org/10.1016/j.jpeds.2021.08.068.

Richards, M. N., & Calvert, S. L. (2017). Media characters, parasocial relationships, and the social aspects of children's learning across media platforms. In R. Barr & D. N. Linebarger (eds.), *Media Exposure during Infancy and Early Childhood: The Effects of Content and Context on Learning and Development* (pp. 141–163). New York: Springer. https://doi.org/10.1007/978-3-319-45102-2_9.

Rideout, V. (2015). *The Common Sense Census: Media Use by Tweens and Teens in America, A Common Sense Media Research Study, United States,*

2015: Version 1. ICPSR – Interuniversity Consortium for Political and Social Research. https://doi.org/10.3886/ICPSR38018.V1.

Rideout, V. (2017). *The Common Sense Census: Media Use by Kids Age Zero to Eight*. San Francisco, CA: Common Sense Media.

Rideout, V., Peebles, A., Mann, S., & Robb, M. B. (2022). *Common Sense Census: Media Use by Tweens and Teens, 2021*. San Francisco, CA: Common Sense Media.

Rideout, V., & Robb, M. B. (2020). *The Common Sense Census: Media Use by Kids Age Zero to Eight, 2020*. San Francisco, CA: Common Sense Media.

Robinson, T. N., Banda, J. A., Hale, L. et al. (2017). Screen media exposure and obesity in children and adolescents. *Pediatrics*, *140*(Supplement 2), S97–S101. https://doi.org/10.1542/peds.2016-1758K.

Robinson, C. A., Domoff, S. E., Kasper, N., Peterson, K. E., & Miller, A. L. (2022). The healthfulness of children's meals when multiple media and devices are present. *Appetite*, *169*, 105800. https://doi.org/10.1016/j.appet.2021.105800.

Roche, E., Rocha Hidalgo, J., Piper, D. et al. (2022). Presence at a distance: Video chat supports intergenerational sensitivity and positive infant affect during COVID-19. *Infancy*, *27*, 1008–1031. doi.org/10.1111/infa.12491.

Rosenblum, K. L., McDonough, S., Muzik, M., Miller, A., & Sameroff, A. (2002). Maternal representations of the infant: Associations with infant response to the still face. *Child Development*, *73*(4), 999–1015. https://doi.org/10.1111/1467-8624.00453.

Roskam, I., Aguiar, J., Akgun, E. et al. (2021). Parental burnout around the globe: A 42-country study. *Affective Science*, *2*, 58–79. https://doi.org/10.1007/s42761-020-00028-4.

Roskam, I., Brianda, M.-E., & Mikolajczak, M. (2018). A step forward in the conceptualization and measurement of parental burnout: The parental burnout assessment (PBA). *Frontiers in Psychology*, *9*, 758. https://doi.org/10.3389/fpsyg.2018.00758.

Rubin, A. M. (1986). Uses, gratifications, and media effects research. In J. Bryant & D. Zillmann (eds.), *Perspectives on Media Effects* (pp. 281–301). Hillsdale, NJ: Lawrence Erlbaum Associates.

Ruysschaert, L., Warreyn, P., Wiersema, J. R., Metin, B., & Roeyers, H. (2013). Neural mirroring during the observation of live and video actions in infants. *Clinical Neurophysiology*, *124*(9), 1765–1770. https://doi.org/10.1016/j.clinph.2013.04.007.

Sadeh, A. (2004). A brief screening questionnaire for infant sleep problems: Validation and findings for an internet sample. *Pediatrics*, *113*(6), e570–e577. https://doi.org/10.1542/peds.113.6.e570.

Sameroff, A. (2010). A unified theory of development: A dialcctic integration of nature and nurture. *Child Development*, *81*(1), 6–22. https://doi.org/10.1111/j.1467-8624.2009.01378.x.

Schmidt, M. E., Pempek, T. A., Kirkorian, H. L., Frankenfield, A. F., & Anderson, D. R. (2008). The effects of background television on the toy play behavior of very young children. *Child Development*, *79*, 1137–1151. https://doi.org/10.1111/j.1467-8624.2008.01180.x.

Schwartz, L., Levy, J., Endevelt-Shapira, Y. et al. (2022). Technologically-assisted communication attenuates inter-brain synchrony. *NeuroImage*, *264*, 119677. https://doi.org/10.1016/j.neuroimage.2022.119677.

Seehagen, S., Konrad, C., Herbert, J. S., & Schneider, S. (2015). Timely sleep facilitates declarative memory consolidation in infants. *Proceedings of the National Academy of Sciences of the United States of America*, *112*(5), 1625–1629. https://doi.org/10.1073/pnas.1414000112.

Sen, A., & Tucker, C. E. (2020). Social Distancing and School Closures: Documenting Disparity in Internet Access among School Children. SSRN 3572922. 2020.

Shawcroft, J., Blake, H., Gonzalez, A., & Coyne, S. M. (2023). Structures for screens: Longitudinal associations between parental media rules and problematic media use in early childhood. *Technology, Mind, and Behavior*, *4*(2: Summer 2023). https://doi.org/10.1037/tmb0000104.

Shin, E., Choi, K., Resor, J., & Smith, C. L. (2021). Why do parents use screen media with toddlers? The role of child temperament and parenting stress in early screen use. *Infant Behavior & Development*, *64*, 101595. https://doi.org/10.1016/j.infbeh.2021.101595.

Strouse, G. A., & Ganea, P. A. (2016). Are prompts provided by electronic books as effective for teaching preschoolers a biological concept as those provided by adults? *Early Education and Development*, *27*, 1190–1204. https://doi.org/10.1080/10409289.2016.1210457.

Strouse, G. A., & Ganea, P. A. (2017). Parent–toddler behavior and language differ when reading electronic and print picture books. *Frontiers in Psychology*, *8*, 677. http://doi.org/10.3389/fpsyg.2017.00677.

Strouse, G. A., McClure, E., Myers, L. J. et al. (2021). Zoom-ing through development: Using video chat to support family connections. *Human Behavior and Emerging Technologies 3*, 552–571. https://doi.org/10.1002/hbe2.268.

Strouse, G. A., O'Doherty, K., & Troseth, G. L. (2013). Effective coviewing: Preschoolers' learning from video after a dialogic questioning intervention. *Developmental* Psychology, *49*, 2368–2382. https://doi.org/10.1037/a0032463.

Strouse, G. A., & Samson, J. E. (2021). Learning from video: A meta-analysis of the video deficit in children ages 0 to 6 years. *Child Development*, *92*(1), e20–e38. https://doi.org/10.1111/cdev.13429.

Suh, B., Kirkorian, H., Barr, R., Kucker, S., Torres, C., & Radesky, J. (2024). Measuring Parents' Regulatory Media Use for Themselves and Their Children. *Frontiers, in Development*. https://doi.org/10.3389/fdpys.2024.1377998.

Sundqvist, A., Barr, R., Heimann, M., Birberg-Thornberg, U., & Koch, F. (2023). A longitudinal study of the relationship between children's exposure to screen media and vocabulary development. *Acta Paediatrica*, apa.17047. https://doi.org/10.1111/apa.17047.

Sundqvist, A., Koch, F., Birberg Thornberg, U., Barr, R., &Heimann, M. (2021). Growing up in a digital world–digital media and the association with the child's language development at two years of age. *Frontiers*, *12*, 569920. https://doi.org/10.3389/fpsyg.2021.569920.

Swedish Media Council (SMC). (2017). Little kids and media. http://statensmedierad.se/publikationer/publicationsinenglish/littlekidsmedia2015.611.html.

Swit, C. S., Coyne, S. M., Shawcroft, J. et al. (2023). Problematic media use in early childhood: The role of parent-child relationships and parental wellbeing in families in New Zealand and the United States. *Journal of Children and Media*, *17*(4), 443–466. https://doi.org/10.1080/17482798.2023.2230321.

Takahashi, I., Obara, T., Ishikuro, M. et al. (2023). Screen time at age 1 year and communication and problem-solving developmental delay at 2 and 4 years. *JAMA Pediatrics*, *177*(10), 1039–1046. https://doi.org/10.1001/jamapediatrics.2023.3057.

Tamis-LeMonda, C. S. (2021). *Child Development: Context, Culture, and Cascades*. Oxford: Oxford University Press.

Thompson, A. L., Adair, L. S., & Bentley, M. E. (2013). Maternal characteristics and perception of temperament associated with infant TV exposure. *Pediatrics*, *131*(2), e390–e397. https://doi.org/10.1542/peds.2012-1224.

Tombeau Cost, K. T., Korczak, D., Charach, A. et al. (2020). Association of parental and contextual stressors with child screen exposure and child screen exposure combined with feeding. *Pediatrics*, *3*, e1920557. https://doi.org/10.1001/jamanetworkopen.2019.20557.

Tomopoulos, S., Dreyer, B. P., Berkule, S. et al. (2010). Infant media exposure and toddler development. *Archives of Pediatrics & Adolescent Medicine*, *164* (12), 1105–1111. https://doi.org/10.1001/archpediatrics.2010.235.

Tomopoulos, S., Dreyer, B. P., Valdez, P. et al. (2007). Media content and externalizing behaviors in Latino toddlers. *Ambulatory Pediatrics: The Official Journal of the Ambulatory Pediatric Association*, *7*(3), 232–238. https://doi.org/10.1016/j.ambp.2007.02.004.

Torres, C., Radesky, J., Levitt, K. J., & McDaniel, B. T. (2021). Is it fair to simply tell parents to use their phones less? A qualitative analysis of parent phone use. *Acta Paediatrica (Oslo, Norway: 1992)*, *110*(9), 2594–2596. https://doi.org/10.1111/apa.15893.

Troseth, G. L. (2010). Is it life or is it Memorex? Video as a representation of reality. *Developmental Review*, *30*(2), 155–175. https://doi.org/10.1016/j.dr.2010.03.007.

Troseth, G. L., Flores, I., & Stuckelman, Z. D. (2019). When representation becomes reality: Interactive digital media and symbolic development. *Advances in Child Development and Behavior*, *56*, 65–108. https://doi.org/10.1016/bs.acdb.2018.12.001.

Twenge, J. M., Krizan, Z., & Hisler, G. (2017). Decrease in self-reported duration among U.S. adolescents 2009–2015 and association with new media screen time. *Sleep Medicine*, *39*, 47–53. https://doi.org/10.1016/j.sleep.2017.08.013.

Valkenburg, P., Beyens, I., Pouwels, J. L., Van Driel, I. I., & Keijsers, L. (2021). Social media use and adolescents' self-esteem: Heading for a person-specific media effects paradigm. *Journal of Communication*, *71*(1), 56–78. https://doi.org/10.1093/joc/jqaa039.

Valkenburg, P. M., Krcmar, M., Peeters, A. L., & Marseille, N. M. (1999). Developing a scale to assess three styles of television mediation: "Instructive mediation," "restrictive mediation," and "social coviewing." *Journal of Broadcasting & Electronic Media*, *43*(1), 52–66. https://doi.org/10.1080/08838159909364474.

Valkenburg, P. M., & Peter, J. (2013). The differential susceptibility to media effects model. *Journal of Communication*, *63*(2), 221–243. https://doi.org/10.1111/jcom.12024.

Valkenburg, P. M., & Peter, J. (2017). Differential susceptibility to media effects model. In P. Rössler, C. A. Hoffner, & L. Zoonen (eds.), *The International Encyclopedia of Media Effects* (*1st ed.*) (pp. 1–6). Hoboken, NJ: Wiley. https://doi.org/10.1002/9781118783764.wbieme0119.

van den Heuvel, M., Ma, J., Borkhoff, C. M. et al. (2019). Mobile media device use is associated with expressive language delay in 18-month-old children. *Journal of Developmental and Behavioral Pediatrics*, *40*(2), 99–104. https://doi.org/10.1097/DBP.0000000000000630.

Vanden Abeele, M. M., Abels, M., & Hendrickson, A. T. (2020). Are parents less responsive to young children when they are on their phones? A systematic naturalistic observation study. *Cyberpsychology, Behavior, and Social Networking*, *23*(6),363–370. https://doi.org/10.1089/cyber.2019.0472.

Vandewater, E. A., & Lee, S. J. (2009). Measuring children's media use in the digital age: Issues and challenges. *The American Behavioral Scientist, 52*, 1152–1176. https://doi.org/10.1177/0002764209331539.

Ventura, A. K., & Teitelbaum, S. (2017). Maternal distraction during breast-and bottle feeding among WIC and non-WIC mothers. *Journal of Nutrition Education and Behavior, 49*(7), S169–S176. https://doi.org/10.1016/j.jneb.2017.04.004.

Ventura, A. K., Sheeper, S., & Levy, J. (2019). Exploring correlates of infant clarity of cues during early feeding interactions. *Journal of the Academy of Nutrition and Dietetics, 119*(9), 1452–1461. https://doi.org/10.1016/j.jand.2019.03.014.

Verlinden, M., Tiemeier, H., Hudziak, J. J. et al. (2012). Television viewing and externalizing problems in preschool children: The generation R study. *Archives of Pediatrics & Adolescent Medicine, 166*(10), 919–925. https://doi.org/10.1001/archpediatrics.2012.653.

Vijakkhana, N., Wilaisakditipakorn, T., Ruedeekhajorn, K., Pruksananonda, C., & Chonchaiya, W. (2015). Evening media exposure reduces night-time sleep. *Acta Paediatrica* (*Oslo, Norway*: *1992*), *104*(3), 306–312. https://doi.org/10.1111/apa.12904.

Vik, F. N., Grasaas, E., Polspoel, M. E. M. et al. (2021). Parental phone use during mealtimes with toddlers and the associations with feeding practices and shared family meals: A cross-sectional study. *BMC Public Health, 21*(1), 756. https://doi.org/10.1186/s12889-021-10757-1.

Wang, M., Lwin, M. O., Cayabyab, Y. M. T. M, Hou, G. & You, Z. (2023). A meta-analysis of factors predicting parental mediation of children's media use based on studies published between 1992–2019. *Journal of Child and Family Studies, 32*, 1249–1260. https://doi-org.proxy.library.georgetown.edu/10.1007/s10826-022-02459-y.

Ward, L. M., Tran-Dubongco, M., Moss, L., & Cox, V. (2020). Media use and the development of racial and ethnic attitudes and stereotypes. In J. van den Bulck, J. (Ed.), *The International Encyclopedia of Media Psychology*. Hoboken, NJ: Wiley-Blackwell. https://doi.org/10.1002/9781119011071.iemp0080.

Warner Schaie, K. (2015). Cohort sequential designs (Convergence analysis). In R. L. Cautin & S. O. Lilienfeld (eds.) *The Encyclopedia of Clinical Psychology*. Hoboken, NJ: Wiley, https://doi.org/10.1002/9781118625392.wbecp098.

Weintraub, S., Dikmen, S. S., Heaton, R. K. et al. (2013). Cognition assessment using the NIH Toolbox. *Neurology, 80*(11 Suppl 3), S54–S64. https://doi.org/10.1212/WNL.0b013e3182872ded.

Wiederhold, B. K. (2020). Children's screen time during the COVID-19 pandemic: Boundaries and etiquette. *Cyberpsychology, Behavior and Social Networking*, *23*(6), 359–360. https://doi.org/10.1089/cyber.2020.29185.bkw.

Willis, E. A., Hales, D., Smith, F. T. et al. (2022). Feasibility and acceptability of wearable sensor placement for measuring screen time of children. *Translational Journal of the American College of Sports Medicine*, *7*(4), e000214. https://doi.org/10.1249/TJX.0000000000000214.

Wolfers, L. N., & Schneider, F. M. (2020). Using media for coping: A scoping review. *Communication Research*, *52*(8), 1152–1176. https://doi.org/10.1177/0093650220939778.

World Health Organization. (2018). Gaming disorder. Accessed online [June 5, 2019] at: www.who.int/features/qa/gaming-disorder/en/.

Wright, J. C., Huston, A. C., Murphy, K. C. et al. (2001). The relations of early television viewing to school readiness and vocabulary of children from low-income families: The early window project. *Child Development*, *72*, 1347–1366. https://doi.org/10.1111/1467-8624.t01-1-00352.

Xu, H., Wen, L. M., Hardy, L. L., & Rissel, C. (2016). Associations of outdoor play and screen time with nocturnal sleep duration and pattern among young children. *Acta Paediatrica (Oslo, Norway: 1992)*, *105*(3), 297–303. https://doi.org/10.1111/apa.13285.

Yuan, N., Weeks, H. M., Ball, R. et al. (2019). How much do parents actually use their smartphones? Pilot study comparing self-report to passive sensing. *Pediatric Research*, *86*(4), 416–418. https://doi.org/10.1038/s41390-019-0452-2.

Zack, E., & Barr, R. (2016). The role of interactional quality in learning from touch screens during infancy: Context matters. *Frontiers in Psychology*, *7*, 1264. http://doi.org/10.3389/fpsyg.2016.01264.

Zhang, Z., Adamo, K. B., Ogden, N. et al. (2022). Associations between screen time and cognitive development in preschoolers. *Paediatrics & Child Health*, *27*(2), 105–110. https://doi.org/10.1093/pch/pxab067.

Zhang, Z., Sousa-Sá, E., Pereira, J. et al. (2019). Correlates of nocturnal sleep duration, nocturnal sleep variability, and nocturnal sleep problems in toddlers: Results from the GET UP! Study. *Sleep Medicine*, *53*, 124–132. https://doi.org/10.1016/j.sleep.2018.08.035.

Zhang, Z., Sousa-Sá, E., Pereira, J. R. et al. (2021). Correlates of sleep duration in early childhood: A systematic review. *Behavioral Sleep Medicine*, *19*(3), 407–425. https://doi.org/10.1080/15402002.2020.1772264.

Zhao, F., Egelman, S., Weeks, H. M. et al. (2020). Data collection practices of mobile applications played by preschool-aged children. *JAMA Pediatrics*, *174*(12), e203345. https://doi.org/10.1001/jamapediatrics.2020.3345.

Zimmerman, F. J., & Christakis, D. A. (2007). Associations between content types of early media exposure and subsequent attentional problems. *Pediatrics*, *120*(5), 986–992. https://doi.org/10.1542/peds.2006-3322.

Zimmerman, F. J., Gilkerson, J., Richards, J. A. et al. (2009). Teaching by listening: The importance of adult-child conversations to language development. *Pediatrics*, *124*, 342–349. https://doi.org/10.1542/peds.2008-2267.

Cambridge Elements

Child Development

Marc H. Bornstein
National Institute of Child Health and Human Development, Bethesda
Institute for Fiscal Studies, London
UNICEF, New York City

Marc H. Bornstein is an Affiliate of the *Eunice Kennedy Shriver* National Institute of Child Health and Human Development, an International Research Fellow at the Institute for Fiscal Studies (London), and UNICEF Senior Advisor for Research for ECD Parenting Programmes. Bornstein is President Emeritus of the Society for Research in Child Development, Editor Emeritus of *Child Development*, and founding Editor of *Parenting: Science and Practice*.

About the Series

Child development is a lively and engaging, yet serious and real-world subject of scientific study that encompasses myriad theories, methods, substantive areas, and applied concerns. Cambridge Elements in Child Development addresses many contemporary topics in child development with unique, comprehensive, and state-of-the-art treatments of principal issues, primary currents of thinking, original perspectives, and empirical contributions to understanding early human development.

Cambridge Elements

Child Development

Elements in the Series

A full series listing is available at: www.cambridge.org/EICD

For EU product safety concerns, contact us at Calle de José Abascal, 56–1°, 28003 Madrid, Spain or eugpsr@cambridge.org.

www.ingramcontent.com/pod-product-compliance
Ingram Content Group UK Ltd.
Pitfield, Milton Keynes, MK11 3LW, UK
UKHW022146080726
473066UK00010B/791

* 9 7 8 1 1 0 8 7 9 4 5 6 5 *